DEAD WOOD

DEAD

The Afterlife of Trees

WOOD

ELLEN WOHL

Oregon State University Press   Corvallis

Cataloging-in-Publication Data is available from the Library of Congress.

ISBN 978-0-87071-527-3 paperback; ISBN 978-0-87071-593-8 ebook

♾ This paper meets the requirements of ANSI/NISO Z39.48-1992 (Permanence of Paper).

First published in 2022 by Oregon State University Press
Printed in the United States of America

Oregon State University
OSU Press

Oregon State University Press
121 The Valley Library
Corvallis OR 97331-4501
541-737-3166 • fax 541-737-3170
www.osupress.oregonstate.edu

Contents

For Annette Wohl, who has long been a connoisseur of dead trees

Of Trees and Rivers

Between every two pines is a doorway to a new world. —John Muir

I have spent my adult life studying rivers. Water simply flowing down a river is actually almost unimaginably complex. Each water molecule follows its own journey, which is anything but simple and straight. Water drags along the rough boundaries of the riverbed and banks, while flow in the center of the river moves swiftly onward. Flow lines diverge like a spreading fan passing across a riffle and then converge and plunge into a pool. The pressure of water flowing downstream forces some of the water into the riverbed at the start of the riffle. Following a slower, subterranean path parallel to the river above, the water eventually returns to the surface and merges once more with the river. Other water seeps into the riverbanks and continues to move downward, joining the groundwater that underlies the river valley.

The movement of water is one instrumental line in a river symphony—perhaps the strings, for the water carries the melody in the sense that it moves everything else in the river. Mineral sediment, from the tiniest particles of clay to the largest boulders, can represent percussion. Certainly, boulders moving downstream during a flood can sound like percussion when you stand on the bank and listen to the deep thunks coming from within the river. Dissolved chemicals and gases such as oxygen in the water might be the wind instruments, their presence not always obvious but of critical importance to sustaining the life of river organisms. Call the organic matter, the dead plants and animals from the tiniest sloughed algal cells and insect carapaces to the largest fallen trees, the brass. Like a trumpet solo, a logjam formed where river flow collects fallen wood creates a forceful addition to the river symphony.

The logjam deflects the flow, scouring a pool to one side or where the water plunges over the jam, and collecting sediment and organic matter in the backwater ponded upstream. Algae grow on the submerged wood. Larval insects come to graze on the algae or to perch on the wood and spread a net woven of their own silk into the current to catch bits of food floating by. The complex spaces among the wood pieces shelter fish from predatory larger fish or raptors.

The sodden wood in the logjam is heavy and individual pieces interlock. Someday a large flood may detach individual pieces or float the entire jam downstream, but the jam might also create such an obstacle that the entire river channel shifts away from it as the jam is gradually buried in sediment and becomes part of the floodplain. Thus, each piece of fallen wood and each logjam adds to the complexity of the river.

While a tree lives it creates shade that keeps the river water cooler and limits the growth of algae on the river's bed. Leaves, needles, bits of bark, seeds—whatever the tree sheds—can enter the river, where microbes and insects use the plant litter as food. The roots of the tree strengthen the riverbanks, limiting the ability of the flowing water to widen the river channel or move it gradually sideways across the floodplain.

How do trees influence rivers? Let me count the ways. I have found that I cannot study rivers without also studying trees. I wrote this book to reflect on and explore the connections between trees and rivers. Plenty of trees grow far away from rivers and never participate in these connections. This book is a tale of river trees, the trees that rely on a river to deposit moist sand and silt in which a tree seed can germinate; open a gap in the canopy through which sunlight can reach seedlings; and leak water to the floodplain soil. Each of the three trees in this book germinates and grows to maturity beside a river. I explore what each of these trees means to the forest ecosystem and to the river, nearshore, and marine ecosystems of which the tree becomes a part after it dies and falls into a river. The book could be titled "a tale of three trees, five rivers, the coast, and the ocean," but that seems excessive.

I do, however, want to tell the tale of each tree as an imagined individual that is enmeshed in an ecosystem, first that of the forest and then that of the river and eventually, for two of the trees, the ocean. Each of the three trees, and every tree, is an individual, but no tree is an island. Each tree depends on a nearly uncountable number of other organisms, from microbes to other trees, for its survival. Each tree in turn supports the life of thousands of other living creatures. In telling a tale that is a biography of each tree, I use that individual tree to represent all the trees that sprout and grow in natural forests and eventually die and join the soil, the rivers, the oceans. I follow the life of each tree on a tour of the connections within and among these ecosystems.

Deep History

Trees and rivers have influenced each other for geologic eons, but rivers came first. Before any photosynthetic organism colonized the land, there were rivers. Flowing water cut channels into the land surface, carrying sediment and dissolved chemicals from the high points of the land down to the oceans. Without the roots of plants twining through the sediment of their banks and strengthening the channel against the force of flowing water, the earliest rivers were broad and shallow, braiding among a multitude of secondary channels. Rivers changed forever when plants colonized the land.

The ancestry of trees as photosynthetic plants reaches far, far back, to the formation of a planet over which the atmosphere swung on a pendulum between oxygen rich and oxygen poor. As early as three billion years ago, one-celled blue-green algae living in the ocean produced oxygen as a waste product. If you imagine Earth's history as a written timeline of events, this one merits huge letters and bold font, for now oxygen starts to accumulate in the atmosphere. Reducing minerals such as iron, which combine with oxygen in the process we know as rusting, consumed much of the oxygen released by the algae and sank to the floor of the wine-red sea as equally red sediments. For an unimaginably long time, the algae exhaled and the iron oxidized, or not, while Earth's atmosphere fluctuated between containing abundant oxygen, or not. Iron deposited on the seafloor during times of low oxygen levels remained black, while iron settling to the seabed in the presence of oxygen turned rust red within a matter of hours. More than two billion years later, banded iron formations of layered black and red rock form the core of every continent. More than a thousand feet thick in places and stretching across hundreds of square miles, they record the start of the ongoing adjustments between living organisms and planet Earth.

The Great Oxygenation Event (always capitalized) marked a major turning point in these adjustments, as oxygen became a permanent presence in the atmosphere 2.33 billion years ago. The "0.33" reflects the continuing improvement of the ability of geologists to pin down the date of this critical change. Oxygen in the atmosphere is something we take for granted, although we may become more aware of it when somehow deprived, such as when swimming underwater. Some living organisms have evolved to survive without oxygen, but it is as though they live in slow motion. Creating energy from food is far more efficient via aerobic metabolism, which requires oxygen, as in our contemporary aerobic exercises. The amount of oxygen in the atmosphere has continued to fluctuate since the GOE, but any level of oxygen permits aerobic metabolism to replace anaerobic metabolism. Efficiency had translated into multicelled organisms by six hundred million years ago—and the rest is history.

Fast-forward on the timeline of Earth's history to the evolution of land plants some 430 million years ago. The idea of animals moving from the ocean onto land—a clear precursor of human existence—fascinates many people. Famous cartoons depict early fish gazing longingly toward the adjacent land. Perhaps less glamorously, the latest evidence suggests that land was first colonized by arthropods. These centipede-like creatures about the size of a crayfish left their footprints on sand dunes some 530 million years ago. They were likely temporary visitors, moving briefly onto the land for specific purposes such as avoiding predators.

The earliest land plants were also rather humble in appearance. Their existence is recorded in fossil spores from mosslike plants living in the wetlands along river channels. But, from small seeds grow mighty trees—by 385 million years ago, river wetlands hosted tree ferns and other woody plants with trunks one hundred feet tall.

The evolution of plants with root systems and then with woody stems was something new under the sun for rivers. The oldest river deposits in the rock record—the geologic term for the history of Earth as preserved in rocks—indicate wide, sandy, braided channels. When the sediment forming stream banks is easy to erode, rivers run wild. Floods readily erode the banks, removing so much sediment that the flowing water is unable to transport the sediment very far. Bars form in the channel, shifting the flow toward the opposite bank, which in turn erodes and leads to formation of a new bar. Soon the flow stretches broad and shallow among a multitude of small channels parting around bars that continually shift their location.

Plants with roots are like police providing crowd control. The roots make the stream-bank sediment harder to erode, and the aboveground portion of the plant creates friction that slows the velocity of streamflow. As plants became more widespread and assumed complex forms with roots, some four hundred million years ago, rivers grew narrower and more sinuous, taking on the meandering form so common today.

The widespread expansion of trees over the next eighty million years added large wood to rivers. Logjams can create such effective obstacles to streamflow that the entire channel moves sideways around the jam or a new channel cuts across the floodplain from flow diverted over the stream banks. Fossil logjams preserved in the rock record correspond to the appearance of relatively narrow, vegetated stream channels that branch and rejoin downstream in an anastomosing pattern.

From the blue-green algae of the early oceans to one-hundred-foot-tall tree ferns dying and piling up in rivers as logjams to the majestic giants that cause people to stare upward in open-mouthed wonder, trees as a group have a long and distinguished lineage. Rivers may be parvenus in comparison to blue-green algae: the oldest known rocks formed in river sediments may date to only 1.6 billion years ago. For at least the past 430 million years, however, the lineage of rivers has been intertwined with the lineage of plants. This is worth remembering.

The Biography of Trees beside a River

The tale of each of the three trees in this book begins with the germination of a seed. Trees, like most organisms, produce far more seeds than necessary to perpetuate the species. An enormous number of pollen grains, the male gametes, end up blown across the landscape and dropped on the ground or into water—everywhere but onto the ovule of a female gamete. Different plant species require specific ranges of air temperature and precipitation to survive, and the pollen grains of each plant species have a distinctive shape. When pollen grains broadcast on the wind settle on the bed of a lake, they create a very nice record of changes in vegetation and climate through time that scientists can interpret by extracting cores of lake sediment. This is great for the scientists but does nothing for the plant producing the pollen. Even the pollen grains that fertilize an ovule and create a potential plant face a challenging future. The majority of seeds that manage to germinate do not live past the first season or two of growth. Fluctuating sunlight, heat, or moisture that stress the plant; getting eaten by insects or larger animals; being outcompeted by other plants—a seedling can meet its end in a variety of ways. Just as surviving childhood was difficult for many people in centuries past, so surviving the seedling phase is a barrier to many seeds growing into trees.

A tree that germinates near a river will be influenced by that river for its whole life and beyond. The moist, fertile soil along the riverbanks helps it germinate, and the river attracts other plants and animals that will affect its growth and survival, from browsing moose to beavers building dams of chewed wood. Erosion by the river topples mature trees and opens the forest canopy. Deposition by the river creates new germination sites for seeds. Mature trees that fall into the river block the flow and form logjams, or start on a long journey downstream, perhaps eventually reaching the ocean as driftwood. The creek or river near the tree is an integral character in each of these tales because trees and rivers have influenced each other for hundreds of millions of years.

Introducing the Three Trees and Their Rivers

The tree of the first tale is an Engelmann spruce (*Picea engelmannii*) growing in the subalpine forest of Rocky Mountain National Park in the US state of Colorado.

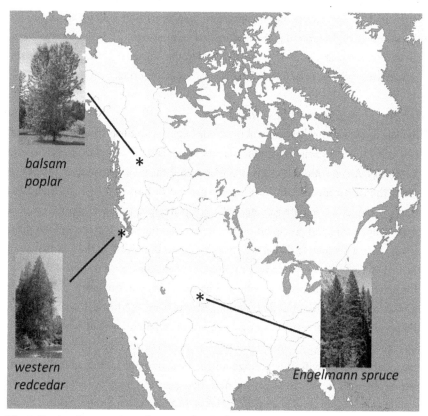

balsam
poplar

western
redcedar

Engelmann spruce

Map indicating the approximate location of each of the three trees, with inset photos of each tree species.

People like names. They give us power, for they imply understanding and perhaps mastery—few people are like the characters in Capote's novel *Breakfast at Tiffany's*, who refer to their house cat as simply "Cat." So, let's spend a minute on names. The genus name *Picea* derives from the Latin *piceus* and *pix*, meaning "pitch" or "sap." The species is named for the nineteenth-century German American botanist Georg Engelmann. The spruce of this tale stands on the floodplain of North St. Vrain Creek, named for nineteenth-century fur trapper Ceran St. Vrain.

Near its beginning at Thunder Lake, the creek is at most thirty feet wide, easily crossed on foot during late summer, but too deep and swift to cross during June's snowmelt peak flow. It descends steeply from its headwaters at 12,000 feet along the Continental Divide to the beaver meadow along the eastern boundary of Rocky Mountain National Park at 8,400 feet. The channel alternately cascades down boulder and log steps and then spreads among multiple channels that branch and rejoin across wider, gentler sections of valley floor. This steep-shallow alternation occurs all the way down the valley to the junction of North and South St. Vrain Creeks beyond the mountain front. The spruce grows in one of the gentler valley sections, and once the tree dies a portion falls into the creek as a logjam and another portion of the dead tree gradually returns to the floodplain in which it germinated. This represents one scenario for a tree that dies in a natural forest where dead wood is not removed.

The second tree is a western redcedar (*Thuja plicata*), an evergreen of the cypress family native to western North America and not actually a true cedar. This tree grows in the valley of the Queets River, which rises on the slopes of Mount Olympus in Olympic National Park on Washington's Olympic Peninsula—obviously, Mount Olympus dominates human perceptions of the landscape—and enters the Pacific Ocean. The river is named for the Quai'tso tribe of Native Americans, one of the Coast Salish tribes that have lived in the region of the river for at least five thousand years. Melting glaciers feed the Queets water and sediment. The Humes, Jeffers, and Queets Glaciers all carve away at the flanks of Mount Olympus as their boulder-laden ice moves downslope. The remnants of broken rock and melted ice flow into the Queets.

The Queets is a much larger river than North St. Vrain Creek and regularly carries large quantities of dead wood downstream, depositing the wood on bars along the channel and carrying some all the way to the coastal beach. After the redcedar dies, it remains in the Queets valley for centuries. The log is alternately collected with other wood in a logjam that is buried by sediment as the channel of the Queets shifts across the floodplain, and then reexposed by new bank erosion and carried farther downstream. This repeated cycle of burial, exhumation, and transport is accompanied by progressive decay and breakage over many centuries, until only fragments of the tree reach the coastal beach. This represents another scenario for a tree that dies in a natural forest.

The third tree is a balsam poplar (*Populus balsamifera*) growing in the valley of the Kechika River, a tributary of the Liard River and ultimately of the Mackenzie River in Canada. The upper tributaries of the Mackenzie rise in southern Canada and then flow north into Great Slave Lake. The Mackenzie itself flows from the lake, more than a thousand miles along the eastern flank of the Rockies to the Arctic Ocean. The *Populus* genus is native in North America as well as Eurasia, and balsam poplar is the northernmost deciduous tree in North America. The name "Kechika" is attributed to a Sikanni Indian word for "big windy." The Sikanni (or Sekani) are an Athabaskan people of northern British Columbia.

The balsam poplar of this tale germinates on a bar of sediment newly deposited by the Kechika River. The poplar is killed more than a century later when the river shifts sideways again and erodes the bar. That is the start of a very long journey for the dead tree, which floats in stages down the Kechika, the Liard, and the Mackenzie Rivers and into the Arctic Ocean. As the tree trunk approaches the ocean, a part is broken off and stored with a huge raft of other wood in the delta of the Mackenzie River. The remainder of the tree moves into the Beaufort Gyre in the Arctic Ocean and eventually drifts all the way to the eastern coast of Greenland. Long-distance oceanic transport and wood sunken on the bed of the ocean represent a third scenario for a tree that dies in a natural forest.

In this tale of three trees, I give as much attention to what happens to the tree after death as to what happens when it is alive. This is partly because many trees last longer as discernible entities after death—distinct logs, even if thoroughly decayed—than they do as a living organism. This emphasis also partly reflects the enormous, but underappreciated, importance of this existence after death. While alive, a tree can support a huge mass of other living organisms. These fellow travelers are insects, bacteria, fungi, and other microorganisms living within and on the tree leaves, branches, trunks, and roots, as well as the more obvious plants growing in the forest canopy—lichens, mosses, vines, bromeliads—and cavity-nesting birds and other animals. Even after the tree itself dies, though, its decaying tissues can support an impressive diversity and cumulative mass of other organisms for many centuries.

The Need for Morticulture

Each of the trees in this tale lives in a forest not directly managed by humans, with no history of commercial timber harvest. After death, each tree falls into an unmanaged river that has no dams, no artificial levees, and no history of removing large wood from the river to facilitate navigation or prevent flooding. Such forests and rivers are almost gone.

People started cutting trees to clear land for crops and provide building materials and fuel more than three thousand years ago in some parts of the world. Since then, we have managed to cut almost half the world's forests. Today, forests cover about a third of the planet's land area, and about a third of those forests are primary forests of native tree species with no history of timber harvest. Rates of deforestation have accelerated since the mid-twentieth century, and now each year we destroy enough of all types of forest to completely cover Belgium.

Deforestation can be measured using satellite imagery, and an online search readily reveals global estimates of total deforested area and contemporary rates of forest destruction. Human alterations of rivers are more covert. Large dams are accurately recorded: as of 2015, about 48 percent of river flow globally was affected by large dams. But how many miles of rivers have we channelized or walled within artificial levees? In the contiguous United States, only 2 percent of total river miles are still relatively natural. Two percent! Those are crisis-level figures. There is no knowing how much large wood has been pulled from rivers around the world to improve navigation or control floods. Using records from the US secretary of war, scientists estimated that more than 1.5 million logs were removed from thirty rivers in the contiguous United States from 1867 to 1912. This is only a partial count for a limited number of one country's rivers.

Once upon a time, people worshipped trees. Sacred groves predate monotheism in ancient Greek, Roman, Celtic, Asian, African, and Native American cultures. Some cultures continue to view designated areas of forest as sacred, and these forests include standing and fallen dead trees. In much of the contemporary world, however, to paraphrase Robert Frost, something there is that doesn't love a dead tree.

People have spent more than a century energetically removing every piece of wood and every logjam that they could from forest floors and river channels. Why? In forests, wood has been harvested for fuels to burn for heat or cooking or generating steam power or, more recently, to limit fuels for wildfires, improve access for industrial-scale timber harvest, or simply make the forest look neater. In rivers, nineteenth-century steamboats had a terrible record of sinking rapidly when a submerged log punched a hole in the hull. Also, the logjams that provide homes and food for so many river creatures can obstruct flow in the channel and force the water over the banks to inundate the floodplain and associated cities and croplands. There are also infrastructure hazards—a wood flood in which thousands of logs rush downstream at high speeds like so many javelins can pile up against a bridge and take it down in less than an hour. As far as aesthetics or recreational fishing, people have not always appreciated the appearance of a river bristling with partly submerged logs, and anglers prefer not to lose lures or flies that get entangled with wood. Not to mention the mistaken perception that logjams can create a barrier to fish movements. For reasons many and various, people have pulled wood from rivers and deforested the floodplains and uplands that might provide wood to the rivers. In the process, we have done a great disservice to the natural world.

To be fair, scientists have come to realize the importance of dead wood only relatively recently. For more than a century, human perceptions of forests have emphasized the importance of living, growing trees. Even old trees, although still alive, have been denigrated, and old-growth forests were once routinely described with derogatory terms such as overmature and decadent. This attitude stemmed from the European, utilitarian perspective of forests as timber-production farms. Gifford Pinchot imported this attitude from Europe to the United States and disseminated it widely during the nineteenth century. Pinchot, an enormously influential forester, was a friend of Theodore Roosevelt and the first head of the US Forest Service. His attempts to regulate forests to more efficiently produce and conserve the supply of trees for timber were partly a reaction to the rapid and wasteful destruction of US forests following European settlement. The first wave of farmers burned forests to clear the trees for crops. The first commercial lumbermen were so anxious to get the most valuable timber that their cutting and log-collecting practices wasted large amounts of timber and left vast clear-cut swaths of land. Pinchot's work eventually translated to a regular cutting cycle in forests subject to timber harvest, as well as strenuous efforts to "clean up"—remove—standing and downed dead wood in forests and rivers.

Similarly, people once worshipped rivers and continue to do so in some parts of the world. Monotheism has largely eliminated worship of natural features, however, and wood removal in rivers to facilitate navigation and reduce over-bank flooding dates back many centuries in Europe and Asia. Wood removal from rivers was practiced energetically starting in the eighteenth century in the United States, Australia, and other regions settled later by Europeans. Wood removal from almost all rivers continues today.

Scientific recognition of the importance of dead wood in forests and streams dates only from the very late 1970s and early 1980s. Much of this understanding grew out of research in a single place: the H. J. Andrews Experimental Forest in western Oregon. The Andrews Forest includes large stands of old-growth trees whose average age exceeds two hundred years. Here, both standing dead trees and downed wood are allowed to remain in place and decay slowly and naturally. A remarkable convergence of scientists studying trees, soil, rivers, hillslopes, birds, invertebrates, mammals, lichens, mosses, climate, fish—everything in the forest—came together at the Andrews during the 1970s and 1980s. Through meticulous research the scientists convincingly demonstrated that, far from being a decadent waste of good timber, an old-growth forest was a wonderland of interconnected processes and biological communities that supported an enormous mass and diversity of living organisms capable of producing every ecosystem service that humans need to survive—clean water, clean air, and fertile soil—continually renewed by the forest ecosystem.

This complete change in scientific understanding of forests has revolutionized societal attitudes. People who may not understand the intricacies of ecosystem functioning nevertheless speak with reverence of the importance and beauty of old-growth forests and, in some cases, risk their lives to protect these forests from logging. The appreciation of aging and decay does not necessarily extend beyond existing old-growth forests, however. Visitors may marvel at the old-growth temperate rain forest of Washington's Olympic National Park or the tropical rain forest of the Amazon River basin or Borneo, but they do not necessarily make the connection that removing downed wood from the neighborhood forest or creek also impoverishes those ecosystems. This is why forest ecologist Mark Harmon, who has spent his career working at the Andrews Experimental Forest, calls for the practice of morticulture. Silviculture—the growing and cultivation of trees—has a long and proud tradition around the world. In the United States, we regularly plant trees for Arbor Day, the April holiday celebrating trees. Planting a tree symbolizes hope, belief in the future, a gift to others that will extend long beyond an individual person's lifetime, and an investment in the natural world. What does leaving a dead tree standing (or fallen) symbolize in western culture? Laziness, indifference, sloppiness?

In a 2001 scientific paper, Harmon proposed that morticulture be given equal attention with silviculture. Morticulture emphasizes managing dead wood to meet the needs of forests as ecosystems rather than as simply timber agriculture. This requires understanding the processes by which wood decays. It also requires knowing how various organisms depend on the amount and arrangement of downed wood. From fungi and wood-boring beetles that live within decaying wood to pine martens that use downed wood for winter resting sites or black bears that tear it apart to get at the termites within, many forest creatures depend on dead wood. The ability of living plants to obtain nitrogen, phosphorus, and other elements vital to their growth and survival also depends greatly on the fungi and microbes colonizing decaying wood. Equally diverse stream organisms, from bottom-dwelling algae and larval aquatic insects through salmonids, use dead wood that falls into streams and rivers. Even a suite of marine creatures, from microbes to crabs to tuna, rely on driftwood reaching the oceans after a long journey down a river.

Ultimately, morticulture means that trees receive as much human attention and care after death as during life. This tale of three trees echoes that idea by extending the tale of each tree's life into the long period after the tree's death to examine the ways in which decaying wood gives rise to other life, sometimes in surprising ways.

The First Tree: Headwaters

The Neighborhood, Writ Large

The Engelmann spruce that is the focus of this tale has an enormous extended family, but they all like it cold. Different species of spruce grow throughout the Northern Hemisphere in mountains and at high latitudes. Those in North America evolved about sixty-five million years ago. Now, Engelmanns cover a broad elevational range, from riparian forests in the foothills up to timberline across western North America, and from northern Mexico to above the Arctic Circle.

With the cold of altitude and latitude come other challenges: wildfires, blow-downs, and tree-killing insects. Just as ancestral history can create a challenging or a favorable environment for a newly born child, so the natural history of a site creates a challenging or a favorable environment for the seed that may grow to a tree. Disasters that kill ancestors may provide opportunities for subsequent generations. A wildfire that killed much of the existing forest provided the opportunity for the spruce of this tale to germinate more than four hundred years ago.

Four hundred years or more can pass between intense wildfires in this forest, but sometimes lightning strikes start an intense crown fire that kills all the trees. For the first year, the landscape is blackened and silent. Wind moves quietly between the widely spaced trunks of trees from which the fire has consumed small branches and needles. The terrain, stripped bare of the undergrowth and forest litter that soften contours, appears rocky and angular. Fire-sculpted, oddly shaped remnants of trunks form slender black pillars with small facets that shine in sunlight. Accumulated litter and duff are consumed or crisped to ash, and sand-sized charcoal fragments that drift before the wind accumulate in small dunes across the forest floor. Ground plants are burned back to a stubbled clump of stems that stands at most a few inches above the ground. Rocks previously partly buried in plant litter now bristle from the hillslopes and the valley floor, revealing just how thin the soil is in this cold, dry region. The newly burned forest seems eerily quiet in summer without birdsong and squirrel chatter. Yet birds return within days once the flames disappear. Chickadees move among the blackened trunks seeking insects. The work of woodpeckers appears as white patches up and down the trunks where the birds have flaked away the charred outer layers to find living insects still inside the wood. Even the pine squirrels who survived the fire in neighboring unburned patches of forest venture back into the terrain of scorched earth, perhaps looking for seed caches that the fire did not completely consume. The first snow melts off dirty gray, and the creek flows turbid with ash and silt flushed from the burned slopes. But grasses and forbs rise from the charred grounds within weeks of the first year's snowmelt, their pale green startlingly bright among the black ash and charcoal.

The fire begins the forest cycle anew. Engelmann spruce and subalpine fir seedlings germinate in the newly opened space in the forest. After about a hundred years, the spruce trees begin to lose the competition for resources. Smaller spruce trees grow more slowly, and fewer spruce seedlings germinate successfully, while the firs steadily keep growing and germinating. But subalpine firs commonly have shorter life spans than spruces. As the firs that took root after the fire reach the age of three hundred years, large numbers of them begin to die. New firs grow up to replace the old giants, but the spruces come into their own as the forest canopy opens slightly. Eventually, both spruces and firs dominate the forest, and young trees of both species grow at the same rate.

The trees that germinated after that long-ago fire now form one of the larger stands of old-growth forest in this part of Colorado. They are the old stalwarts, survivors despite the odds. Much of their wider community was destroyed by the people of European descent who came to the region hungry for wood starting in 1859. Wood to burn for heating and cooking, wood to build houses and stores, wood to timber mine shafts, wood to support railroad tracks; wood, wood, wood—the insatiable human demand nearly deforested the entire region. Only relatively small pockets of trees survived to bear witness to what had once been.

One of these pockets lies at an elevation of around ten thousand feet in the subalpine forest along North St. Vrain Creek in Rocky Mountain National Park. The Continental Divide bisects the park from north to south, separating the rainfall and snowmelt that will gradually move downslope into the headwaters of the Colorado River and the Pacific Ocean on the western side from the precipitation that moves into the headwaters of the South Platte River and eventually the Atlantic Ocean on the eastern side. The waters of North St. Vrain Creek are destined for the Atlantic, but along the way they nourish the spruce growing beside the creek.

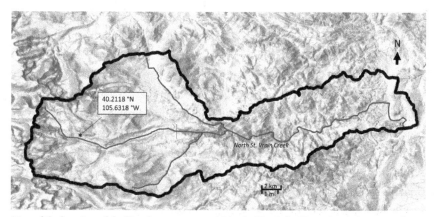

Map of the location of the Engelmann spruce within the North St. Vrain Creek drainage. The heavy line indicates the watershed divides for North St. Vrain Creek. The asterisk indicates the location of the spruce in this tale. The vertical line across the creek at center left indicates the eastern boundary of Rocky Mountain National Park. The creek flows beyond the map at right to enter the Great Plains and join the South Platte River.

The spruce thrives beside the creek because of the relative abundance of water in an otherwise dry land. Warm air carrying moisture moves up from the Gulf of Mexico, hurling down the fierce rains of summer when the air rises over the Rockies. Much of the moisture is wrung from the rising air at the lower elevations of the foothills and montane zone, leaving relatively little summer rainfall for the higher subalpine and alpine zones. The situation is reversed in winter, when cooler air flows eastward from the Pacific and drops snow predominantly on the higher elevations, creating greater precipitation totals there. Eastward-moving air from the Pacific rises first over the Coast Ranges and then over the broad, corrugated topography of all the individual ranges that together constitute the Rocky Mountains. By the time the air reaches the eastern edge of the mountains in Colorado, most of the moisture has been wrung out and the snow falls as dry powder. This delights skiers but yields less meltwater than snow on the western coast of the continent.

The valleys that host spruce are a little wider than they might be if only flowing water had carved them. Four times during the past two million years the climate cooled enough to allow winter snows to remain throughout the year at high elevations. Falling snow accumulated in cupped depressions near the Continental Divide, consolidating under the weight of overlying snow and recrystallizing into ice that spilled from each cup and flowed down the nearest river valley as a glacier. Sediment frozen into the ice and dragged along scraped the underlying bedrock. The freezing and thawing of meltwater beside the glacier shattered the rock of the valley walls. Together, the abrasion and freezing cycles widened the glaciated valleys into troughs that stepped down the mountains in alternating flats and drops.

Ten thousand years ago, the air grew warmer and the glaciers melted. Rivers flowed down the widened valleys. Rivers of air followed the valleys, too. Just as the drop over a boulder step froths a creek to turbulent white water, the steep mountain topography of the Rockies froths a river of air to downdrafts and microbursts. "Froths" is probably too gentle a word, though. Gale-force winter winds blast over the mountain peaks and then roar down the slopes, snapping huge tree trunks like toothpicks. Microbursts slam into the valley floor and send a shock wave radiating out in all directions, ripping out entire trees, roots, and chunks of attached soil. Decades pass between the biggest blowdowns, but every winter some trees in the forest fall. Their demise opens the canopy, allowing more sunlight to reach the forest floor and creating newly fallen logs that gradually release the vital nitrogen, carbon, and phosphorus stored in living wood.

The fingerprints of fire and wind are all over the subalpine forest where the spruce of this tale germinates along the banks of North St. Vrain Creek. The seed falls in a forest stand where the oldest trees germinated before 1650 AD. These old trees extend less than three miles along the valley in a band at most half a mile wide. The old-growth forest ends downstream where an extensive wildfire in 1880 reset the forest clock. The trees in the neighboring drainage are just starting to regrow from a fire in 1978. Scattered among the oldest trees are many youngsters that sprang up when wind or insects killed one or a few of the old giants.

This is the ancestral history of the Engelmann spruce and its neighborhood: Glaciers and rivers sculpting the bedrock of the mountains to create a broader, more gently sloping portion of a high-elevation valley that collects sediment in which a seedling can germinate. Winds and fires blasting and burning holes in the forest carpeting the terrain, allowing more sunlight to penetrate in the tattered portions and support the growth of saplings. And a seed dropping in just the right spot.

The Engelmann spruce seed in this tale drops onto the floodplain of North St. Vrain Creek. The creek starts in Thunder Lake, where the jagged peaks that form the Continental Divide snag the passing moist winds, collecting clouds and birthing thunderstorms. Above the lake waters on three sides rise slopes of sand-colored granite partly mantled by fallen rock and talus slopes. The bowl of the lake opens to a broad lip at the south end, and the summer overflow keeps this sunny valley floor covered in sedges and shrubby willows tolerant of being submerged. Within half a mile, though, the broad valley folds tightly onto itself and the creek drops into a steep, narrow valley lined with spruce and fir trees. The channel drops steadily and swiftly down, cascading over huge boulders and bedrock waterfalls. Any tree that falls into the channel may remain in place for a few seasons, but as its branches and upper portion break and the tree becomes a smoothly tapering cylinder of wood, the snowmelt flows hurry the log downstream to the first wider, gentler section of the valley. Here logs pile into jams that split the creek into several channels branching across the valley floor, until a narrower portion of the valley downstream collects them once more into a single channel. The logjams that split the creek also help force the creek waters over the banks and across the valley floor, creating a moist soil rich in nutrients. The seed of this tale drops to the forest floor in one of the valley's wider portions.

Thunder Lake, the headwaters of North St. Vrain Creek, in midsummer. The creek flows from the lake through the marshy terrain in the foreground before coalescing into a steep, narrow channel.

Germination and Seedling

Like every other form of sexual reproduction, a germinating seed represents a winner in the first stage of an ongoing lottery. Each of the three species of tree in these tales relies on the wind to disperse its pollen. That is one strategy for plant reproduction: produce uncountable masses of pollen grains each year, then release them into the air and leave them to their fate—mostly.

Trees have evolved adaptations to ensure that at least some pollen grains land on receptive female reproductive parts. Engelmann spruces hedge their bets by including both male and female reproductive organs on each tree. Strobili—a fancy name for tiny cones—form in spring. "Strobili" comes from the ancient Greek word *strobilos*, "whirlwind," presumably in reference to the spiraled appearance of the strobili, rather than their behavior. The spruce limits the chance of its male conelets fertilizing its own female conelets by bearing the scarlet, erect, female strobili in the upper crown and the purple pendants of its male strobili in the lower crown. The male conelets ripen in late spring to early summer and release their pollen to the wind. If the pollen grains land on a receptive female conelet, fertilization occurs and the conelet rapidly grows to the size of a mature cone.

An Engelmann spruce may start growing cones when it is only five feet tall and a juvenile of 15 to 40 years, but seed production really kicks in when the tree is larger and older—say, 150 to 250 years old. Even then, not all years are equally productive. Good seed crops come every two to five years, when one hundred thousand to more than five hundred thousand spruce seeds may drop onto every acre of forest floor. That sounds like more than hedging your bets, but the newly fallen seeds face a hazardous future.

A spruce cone and branch tip resting on the forest floor among fallen needles from other conifers.

A cone is a suit of armor for seeds, but at some point, the seeds must be released if they are to germinate. By late summer to early autumn the cone ripens, opens, and sheds its seeds. The cone has now served its purpose and may drop from the tree during the following winter or remain attached to the tree for some time.

Seed season for the tree is food season for others. Before the cones even release the seeds, more than a quarter of the seeds can be consumed by spruce seedworms and larval flies. Pine squirrels move through the canopy cutting cones and branch tips that drop to the forest floor in a pine-scented rain of greenery. Stripping seeds and scales from the cones, a squirrel leaves the central stem bare as a corncob sitting on a mound of scales. The leavings from generations of squirrels create a thick pile at the base of selected trees, and in this mound the squirrels bury seeds for later consumption. Small mammals of the forest floor seek out the seeds that ripen and drop on their own from the protective covering of the cone. Deer mice, red-backed mice, mountain voles, chipmunks, and other rodents sustain their own lives on the nutrients that the spruce has packed into its seeds.

Cones start to open in September, and although some seeds continue to fall throughout the winter, most of the seeds have been released by the end of October. Squirrels and other small mammals transport some of them, but most of the small, winged cores of future plants fly on the wind. Nearly half fall within one hundred feet of the parent tree, although a few travel as far as six hundred feet away. Any seeds left through the winter may well travel farther: winter winds can average fifty miles per hour in the subalpine forest, with gusts blasting through at ninety miles an hour.

At ten thousand feet, winter must first be gotten through before the seed that has fallen on the floodplain of North St. Vrain Creek can germinate. Overnight winter temperatures commonly drop well below freezing in the subalpine, but a sheltering mantle of snow insulates the waiting seeds from these extreme low temperatures. Snow gradually fills in the depressions in the valley as ice starts to seal the creek. By January or February, the channel is only a slight depression in the undulating whiteness of the valley floor. No glimpse or murmur of flowing water betrays the movement that continues below the ice. But for the ever-present wind or the single croak of a raven, the forest is mostly silent.

Each morning reveals new patterns of tracks across the snow, from the delicate imprints of rodents and songbirds to the heavy, dragging steps of moose or elk. After a few days with no fresh snowfall, the crisscrossing tracks of snowshoe hares become so numerous that the forest might be the setting for a hare party. Clumped tracks—fore and hind paws together and then a big space to the next clump—record the flexing muscles of the hare propelling the animal in broad leaps across the deep, soft snow.

A snowshoe hare in its summer pelt of light brown fur and snow-white feet.

Chunks of reddish bark and pale wood littering the snow at the base of a tree reveal where a woodpecker has been at work, and the rapping of a sharp bill on wood reverberates through the forest between gusts of wind. The forest animals are quieter than in summer, though. Small numbers of chickadees still fuss at one another, but the other songbirds are gone or silent, and even the vociferous pine squirrels move among the trees without calling attention to themselves.

Viable spruce seeds that survive the winter start to germinate when the snow melts and the air temperature climbs to 45°F. At most, only a quarter of the seeds that reach the ground will germinate, but the seeds are catholic in their tastes. A seed can take root on the duff and litter shed by surrounding plants. Decaying wood on the forest floor provides concentrated nutrients. A seed germinating on the mound of mineral soil turned up by the toppling of a mature tree may have less competition for space and nutrients. Whatever the substrate, stable soil moisture and full shade over about half the nearby ground aid the growing plant. Still, many seedlings die. Like a human child in the era before routine vaccinations, a seedling may find its first few years fraught with perils.

The intense sunlight of high elevations can heat the ground surface and dry both the seedling and the surrounding soil if the seed has germinated in a site with too much sunlight. The roots of spruce seedlings are slow to penetrate the ground and access the soil moisture at greater depths. This makes the seedlings more susceptible to girdling, which kills many tiny spruces in their first five years. Girdling is the death of phloem, the vascular tissue that transports the sugars produced during photosynthesis. The tiny spruce seedlings, lacking a protective outer layer of thick bark and growing close to the soil surface, where temperatures can exceed 100°F on summer days (even when air temperatures never reach 80°F), are particularly susceptible to girdling caused by drought and heat. A strong late summer drought can kill all the year's seedlings if they lose the race to send their roots downward faster than the soil is drying.

The seedling is likely to live or die by the rain that falls during its first growing season, and either too little or too much can be lethal. The intense summer thunderstorms of the Rockies can create rain that mostly runs off the surface without penetrating the soil, or that carries soil along and buries or uncovers seedlings on bare soil surfaces. This is where neighbors matter. Understory plants such as shrubby willows, shrubby cinquefoil, fireweed, and dwarf whortleberry stabilize the soil surface and compete less aggressively for soil moisture. Spruce seedlings that germinate in their vicinity are more likely to survive. Clumps of grasses, sedges, or plants such as mountain bluebells, currants, and Oregon grape, on the other hand, compete for moisture and smother spruce seedlings under their dormant dried leaves and stems when snow blankets the forest floor.

Then there are the other extremes. Frost can occur during any month of the growing season in the valley along North St. Vrain Creek. Newly germinated spruce seedlings are particularly susceptible to early autumn frosts. September in this valley can make you feel glad to be alive. Aspen leaves glow golden and orange as though lit from within, the air is just pleasantly warm, and the sky is azure. But the setting sun abruptly drains the warmth, and frost penetrates the ground surface overnight. Ice crystals on and just beneath the soil surface heave up the ground, ripping out the weak, shallow roots of a spruce seedling. Even after their first year, seedlings remain vulnerable to frost early in the growing season, when ice crystals can damage shoot tissue during freezing and thawing. A heavy late frost can kill all the seedlings from the previous summer.

Other living creatures from the tiniest insects to the largest ungulates can kill the spruce seedlings. Gray-headed juncos clip the tender bits of fresh growth. Insects and rodents eat the plants. Deer, elk, and moose trample and browse the tiny seedlings. Like fish schooling in the ocean to avoid predators, the numerous seeds germinating in a limited area may help some seedlings survive the many hungry mouths that seek them out.

Careful accounting by plant scientists indicates that an average of 665 viable seeds result in one first-year seedling. A whopping 6,800 seeds are needed on average to result in a seedling four or more years old. These numbers come from a clear-cut site. The numbers go down substantially for the most favorable conditions of a shaded, moist site with a northern aspect: only 18 viable seeds are needed to produce a first-year seedling under these conditions, and 32 seeds to produce a five-year-old. On a south-facing site, numbers rise again: 156 seeds for a one-year-old and 341 seeds for a five-year-old. The bottom line: many germinate but few survive.

A seed that germinates is drawing on a gift from the parent trees and on what it can glean from the surroundings. Carbohydrates stored in the seed itself are the parental gift. The seedling is too young to grow needles and produce energy through photosynthesis, so these carbohydrates are vital for initial growth. The environment supplies water to fuel the growth that breaks through the seed shell and creates roots, along with a steady supply of oxygen that supports the tiny plant's ability to turn stored carbohydrate fuels into energy. The growing roots spread into the soil, building a foundation for the future tree. Soil fungi quickly start to grow on and within the growing roots. This sounds as though it could be bad news for the plant—there's a fungus among us. But these fungi are crucial to the growing seedling's survival because they chemically alter nitrogen and phosphorus within the soil in a way that makes these nutrients available to the plant. As the roots develop, they start to release cytokinin, an enzyme that controls the growth of the tree. Aboveground, the growing seedling develops a stem, branches, and needles, and photosynthesis begins.

Unlike an animal, which acquires energy for survival through one point on its body—the mouth—plants acquire energy for survival and growth from above and from below. Above is the atmosphere and photosynthesis. Below is the complex world of the soil in which live nearly invisible fungi that enhance a plant's ability to acquire nutrients through its roots. Whether the energy comes from above or below, the plant's ability to "eat" is completely dependent on the availability of basic elements such as carbon and nitrogen in the surrounding environment; on internal chemical reactions within the plant; and on other organisms living within the plant. Life is not simple for a plant.

Let's start with above. Photosynthesis is alchemy—light energy is turned into chemical energy that can be released to fuel the plant's metabolism. First comes energy from sunlight, absorbed by chlorophyll held inside cells in the spruce needles. Some of the energy is used to strip electrons from water, producing oxygen as a waste product. Hydrogen freed during the splitting of water goes into creating short-lived, high-energy compounds that are the first step in a series of chemical transformations in which carbon dioxide from the atmosphere is added to other carbon compounds to create carbohydrates such as sugars. Carbohydrates represent long-term food stores for plants, to be drawn on when conditions get tough, such as winter temperatures too low for photosynthesis.

There are multiple points of potential weakness in photosynthesis, including the need to obtain carbon dioxide from the atmosphere. Plants obtain carbon dioxide through their stomata, which are tiny pores in the outer layers of leaves and stems. In photographs taken with scanning electron microscopes, a stoma resembles a mouth, and like a mouth, an open stoma loses water vapor. Plants typically close their stomata when the weather is hot and dry, which means they cannot take in the carbon dioxide needed for photosynthesis. This is one reason spruces do better in shaded, moist conditions.

Meanwhile, the rhizosphere below makes equally important contributions to plant survival. The rhizosphere is named from the Greek word *rhiza*, "root." The rhizosphere, a.k.a. the wood-wide web, is the relatively thin but vital layer of soil in which plant roots, fungi, and microorganisms create such a complicated and mutually dependent ecosystem that it deserves to be designated a "sphere," analogous to the atmosphere. Much of the action occurs in the upper layers of soil that are rich in decomposing plant litter—sloughed bark, needles, cones, and other discarded plant parts.

In this subterranean sphere, plant roots are the coral reefs of the soil's open ocean, the biodiversity hot spots where everything happens and (almost) everyone lives. Plant roots secrete proteins and sugars and slough off dead cells, all of which feed fungi, bacteria, and other soil microorganisms. Some of these soil microbes live within the plant roots. Among these are nitrogen-fixing bacteria that chemically signal their presence to the plant—like expected and welcome guests ringing the doorbell—and then colonize root nodules.

Nitrogen is a critical nutrient that most plants cannot live without, but plants cannot obtain nitrogen on their own. Instead, they rely on bacteria that can chemically transform, or "fix," nitrogen into a form accessible by plants. Many species of bacteria perform this critical function. Some live in soil, some in water, and others within plants.

Bacteria in the rhizosphere that take up residence in root nodules live on nutrients from the plant, but they also convert nitrogen gas into a form that can be used by the plant. Ectomycorrhizal fungi, commonly abbreviated as EM fungi, take their name from the Greek *ektos*, "outside," *mykes*, "fungi," and *rhiza*. EM fungi completely sheathe the fine tree roots and take over the supply of water and mineral nutrients, while the tree supplies nutrients manufactured during photosynthesis. Other, free-living, bacteria in the rhizosphere just outside the roots of plants also fix nitrogen into a form that plants can access. Rhizosphere fungi and bacteria also pay for their plant supper by controlling pathogenic microbes that could harm or kill the plants.

Plant growth is limited by the availability of nitrogen and phosphorus. Plants without EM fungi can take up nitrogen released by other fungi, but EM fungi living within a plant significantly increase its ability to obtain nitrogen from anywhere the element is present. One such potential source is rock. As EM fungi go about their lives, they excrete waste products, just like any living organism. Think of it as fungal pee. Fungal pee is rich in organic acids. As it percolates down through the soil into fractures in the underlying bedrock, it partly dissolves the minerals of the rock, making phosphorus and nitrogen available to the adjacent plant roots.

Like the other WWW, the wood-wide web functions as an information superhighway. Roots and their microbial and fungal communities transfer information via chemicals that can inhibit pathogens or plant competitors for resources. Chemical transfer throughout the rhizosphere can also support adjacent plants of the same species, or even other species, that are suffering from stresses such as nutrient deficiencies or insect attack. Consider that for a moment: plants of different species may help one another. Old, dominant trees with abundant sun exposure can function as nurse trees for seedlings growing in their shade by supplying nutrients through subterranean EM bridges between the old tree and the youngsters.

Mycorrhizal networks can connect two or more plants. Older plants have had time to develop a more diverse fungal community in their roots. As many as fifty different species of EM fungi can colonize one host plant, with each fungal species finding its niche in the rhizosphere based on the host plant and differences in soil texture and moisture. When a youngster starts to grow in the forest, these established mycorrhizal communities can move into the roots of the seedling via the fungal network. It's as if you moved into a completely unknown city and a long-established resident immediately shared with you all the knowledge and connections that would allow you to thrive there. Research in forest stands with multiple Douglas-fir trees also indicates that mycorrhizal networks can provide a conduit for transferring water, carbon, and nutrients among plants. In a sense, the entire forest stand becomes a single biological entity because of the subterranean connections created by the fungi.

EM fungi colonize a seedling over the course of the seedling's first year, but the diversity of EM fungi increases as the plant ages. And, not all EM fungi function equally well. Experimental planting of Engelmann seedlings in a forest clear-cut revealed that seedlings colonized by one species of EM fungus could accumulate more nitrogen than seedlings colonized by a different species. Here is where older trees can help create a more supportive environment, because the wood-wide web helps supply seedling roots with EM fungi already established in nearby mature tree roots.

How do the fungi establish in the soil to begin with? Some insight comes from sites that are transitioning from a wet meadow to a drier environment in which conifers can survive. When beavers build dams along a stream, floods are more likely to overtop the channel banks, spread across the floodplain, and infiltrate slowly, helping to create a continually wet soil across the valley floor. Conifers cannot survive in these conditions, but deciduous plants such as willows thrive. If the beavers disappear for some reason, the dams fall into disrepair and the soil gradually dries. The valley floor can remain a grassland for decades, however, still inhospitable to conifers despite the drier soil. The conifers cannot gain a roothold until something introduces EM fungi. That something can be a small, burrowing mammal, such as a southern red-backed vole. Voles like to eat EM fungi and at least some species of fungi like to be eaten, in the sense that their spores germinate more readily after passing through the digestive tract of a small mammal. As voles move from the edge of a conifer forest into an adjacent dry grassland, they disperse fungal spores through their feces: vole poop inoculates the grassland with EM fungi, allowing conifer seedlings to colonize the grassland. When beavers abandon a site along North St. Vrain Creek, this inoculation by vole poop helps Engelmann spruce colonize the floodplain.

At least five years must pass before the seedling spruce can really become established, and even after that, its survival depends on enough soil moisture, cool temperatures, and shade. Growth is slow at the high-elevation site along North St. Vrain Creek. The roots may penetrate only three to four inches during the first year, and the seedling seldom grows taller than an inch. After five years, the plant may still only be three inches tall, and after ten years only eight inches tall.

Growth starts to accelerate after ten years, so that the young tree may reach five feet in height after twenty to forty years, depending on light levels at the forest floor. In the heavy shade of a closed forest canopy, however, a tree five feet tall may be 120 years old. Think about that the next time you go into a national forest to cut a Christmas tree that you will use for perhaps a month.

Although slow to start, a spruce keeps going. Survivors become one of the largest trees at high elevations. The tree matures at about three hundred years and can live for six hundred years, attaining an impressive girth as trunk diameter exceeds three feet at the three-hundred-year mark. But this is getting ahead of the tale.

Sapling

The spruce seedling, like an herbaceous plant, is all primary tissue—no wood. As the seedling grows, a layer of meristematic cells starts the process of turning the seedling into a woody plant. Just as stem cells in a human can specialize as they develop into anything from muscle cells to brain cells, so meristematic cells in plants can produce many different types of cells as they grow and divide. "Meristem" derives from the Greek word *meristós*, meaning "to divide," in recognition of the critical role of these cells in organizing a tree.

As the spruce seedling transitions to a sapling, meristematic cells organize the plumbing of the plant stem. A plant's plumbing consists of xylem, which conducts water, and phloem, which conducts nutrients. These structures form within the vascular cambium. The cambium is conducting tissue within the inner bark of the tree, where water and nutrients are shuttled between leaves and roots and where the tree thickens as it grows. As the seedling becomes a sapling, cells within the cambium connect columns of vascular tissue to form a complete cylinder around the stem. Cells further differentiate into those arranged parallel to the long axis of the tree trunk and those oriented perpendicular to the trunk. Those parallel to the trunk conduct water and nutrients, whereas the perpendicular cells strengthen the trunk and shuttle nutrients from the phloem to the inner xylem. Like the thick, membranous tissue in a human baby's skull that is replaced as the bones grow together after birth, the soft tissue of a seedling transforms into the firm girders of a sapling and then a mature tree as the cells differentiate into woody tissue.

When conditions are good, or at least average, the tree grows far more water-carrying xylem cells than phloem cells. The phloem cells also typically function for only a year, whereas the xylem cells can operate for several years before becoming heartwood. By creating more xylem cells than needed each year, the tree ensures a margin of safety for water transport so that the stomata can remain open for photosynthesis without desiccating the tree. When conditions become stressful, new xylem production may stop, while at least some phloem tissue continues to form.

By the time we humans see the first signs of water stress in a plant—browning of leaves or needles, defoliation of branch tips—things are bad for the plant. Distress signals start well before we commonly notice them. Forest ecologist David Haskell writes in *The Songs of Trees* of using an ultrasonic sensor to eavesdrop on the twig of a ponderosa pine. He describes relative quiet when the twig is well supplied by water, and vigorous acoustic activity as limited water supply from the roots causes the thin strands of water moving upward within the plant's vessels to break. As the flow of water fails, minuscule air pockets explode inside the ponderosa's cells. Haskell describes these ultrasonic snaps as the sounds of mounting distress because air pockets block the flow of water within the tree. He writes, "The forest sizzles, but our ears fail us." The growing spruce's extra xylem cells can help create a margin of safety for just such wear and tear incurred in the arduous process of pulling water from the soil up to the outermost part of the tree's crown.

The growing spruce sapling also begins to branch, assuming the characteristic conifer shape of a well-defined trunk with smaller lateral branches. The junction of each branch with the trunk can form an irregularity in the annual growth layers of the tree. This Engelmann spruce living in the strongly seasonal climate of the Colorado Rocky Mountains has an annual growth cycle in which the cambium becomes active each spring, creating new layers of tissue that will result in the addition of a layer to the tree's circumference. Eventually, these layers form a bull's-eye pattern of annual rings that record the tree's personal history. Good years produce wider rings. Stressful years leave narrow rings. I have seen more than one museum display based on a cross section cut from an old tree, with various events in human history connected to particular tree rings—the US Declaration of Independence is signed, the Civil War is fought, and so forth. We might just as well create a display interpreting the rings from the perspective of the tree's biography: the year of the great fire, the decade of sustained drought, the years of beetles and more beetles.

Even as the sapling grows, it begins to die. Only the youngest wood within a tree carries water and nutrients throughout the plant. This inner bark and sapwood remain alive. As the sapling adds annual growth layers, resins and tannins invade the older heartwood at the center of the trunk and these cells die. Dead does not mean useless, however: the heartwood can provide structural strength for the tree and help retard attacks from infections that might kill it.

Growth of woody tissue also means development of bark. Tree bark consists of multiple layers, analogous to the layers within human skin. Outside the vascular cambium the tree has inner bark composed of secondary phloem, which usually remains functional for only a year, and the cork cambium, which forms in older phloem cells. The layer visible at the surface of the trunk is the outer bark, a layer of dead phloem and cork cells that may flake off each year or remain on the tree for many years.

Bark forms the trunk's first line of defense. It minimizes water loss from the trunk, deters insects and fungi, and protects against fire and mechanical damage such as the force of an adjacent falling tree. Bark is also one of the more distinctive signatures of a tree and facilitates identification. The bark of a mature Engelmann spruce is dark gray and flaky, and thin relative to the diameter of the trunk. Like an older human, an older tree may have a lot of hard bark on it.

As the sapling spruce develops the inner differentiation that produces woody tissue, its roots are also changing. The weak taproot grown by a seedling Engelmann spruce does not survive beyond the juvenile stage. Tree roots can grow deep or broad, depending on soil depth and moisture. This spruce growing in the shallow, moist soil along North St. Vrain Creek goes for breadth, retaining the weak layer of shallow roots that it grew as a seedling. Most of these roots are in the first twelve to eighteen inches of soil. That's about all the soil there is at this site. Deeper lies fractured bedrock, and although tree roots can and do penetrate these fractures, that's a tougher route than growing in soil.

More needles are added as the sapling branches and grows taller. Although the phrase "spruce is spiky" reflects the pointedness of the needle tips, the needles reveal an intricate architecture when examined closely. The season's new needles are a pale bluish green with subtle ridges and grooves parallel to the length of the needle. In cross section, the needle is four sided. The surface architecture, however, barely hints at the world within.

Needles are the spruce's leaves. Each needle is a photosynthetic factory attached to the stem at the petiole. The petiole is the gatekeeper between the needle and the rest of the tree. Vascular tissue in the petiole regulates the flow of water and carbohydrates between the needle and the stem.

A needle, rather than a broad, thin leaf, reflects a way to survive under relatively dry conditions. The surface of the needle is covered with wax and a layer of naturally occurring polyester material known as the cuticle. The wax and cuticle protect the stomata from drying. The stomata are small and sunken below the needle surface, as though shrinking from the harsh dryness of the surrounding air. Needle cells also have thicker walls than cells in broad-leaved trees, making the needle surface hard. Beneath the hard, waxy surface of the needle, the inner tissue contains tiny, membrane-bound sacs of chloroplasts, packed with molecules of chlorophyll that convert light energy to chemical energy. The do-or-die process of evolutionary adaptation has designed the needle like a suit of armor to protect the vital stomata and photosynthetic cells of the spruce.

Closed stomata conserve water. Overnight temperatures below 39°F retard the opening of the stomata the next day, so not as much photosynthesis or water loss occurs during winter. The spruce must be able to open its stomata, however, during the growth season of early spring to late autumn. Engelmann spruces do not hoard water as effectively as some other conifers, and the open stomata lose water. A spruce's relative extravagance with water partly reflects the fact that the trees are rich in needles. A spruce has so many needles that the cumulative surface area of the greenery—and the associated plethora of stomata—is much greater relative to the size of the tree trunk than on other trees that grow nearby. This leads to much greater rates of water loss in spruces than are experienced by similarly sized, adjacent trees of other species. The spruces that thrive are those growing in moist sites that provide enough water to support their profligate water loss through their stomata.

On one hand, growing the cuticle for a needle requires energy and production of carbon via photosynthesis. On the other hand, each needle may remain on the spruce for a decade, rather than falling each autumn as the leaves of deciduous trees do. While it remains on the tree, the needle can also develop its own miniature community. Conifers grow mostly on thin soils and in dry climates that are not particularly ideal for plant growth. The rhizosphere is critical in helping conifers obtain nutrients and survive environmental stresses. A second microscopic community that helps the huge plants survive is even more cryptic: bacteria living in conifer needles.

Endophytes (from the Greek *endon*, "within," and *phuton*, "plant") are organisms that live within a plant. Examine any part of a plant's interior closely and bacteria are likely to be there—they live in the interior of plant roots, stems, needles, and seeds. Endophytic bacteria in Engelmann spruce needles, like EM fungi in the roots, help the spruce fix nitrogen in a form that the plant can use. Engelmann spruces in Colorado host multiple bacterial species in their needles, but a type of bacteria able to fix nitrogen is particularly common. The bacteria present in a spruce needle might simply reflect the species able to survive in such an environment, but the bacteria can also stimulate plant growth and help protect against disease, as well as enhance the plant's acquisition of nitrogen. When scientists grow Engelmann seedlings with and without these bacteria, those seedlings with needle bacterial communities acquire much more nitrogen through their needles. How do the bacteria get there? Many species in the needles are also present in the soil, so scientists assume that the bacteria either move through the plant or blow about in the air and colonize needles from the atmosphere. Either way, the growing sapling thrives to the degree that it can develop its own, interior ecosystems.

Maturity

When does a spruce sapling become a tree? When it is more than three feet tall; when its bark develops a rough texture rather than being smooth; when its trunk becomes less flexible; when its stem reaches some minimum diameter; when it is sexually mature and starts to develop cones and seeds—experts disagree on the definition. Whenever it officially becomes a tree, the spruce will continue growing. Most Engelmann spruces reach heights of 80 to 130 feet, with exceptional individuals topping out at just over 200 feet. That's an achievement because of the associated plumbing and mechanical strength required to grow that tall.

Plumbing involves getting water and nutrients between different portions of a plant. The bridges of the rhizosphere can transfer nutrients between individual plants, but there is also a lot of work in moving materials within one plant. Mostly, water is pulled up from the roots by water lost through the needles. Water molecules in trees, just like water molecules anywhere else, adhere to each other under tension. Open stomata on the needles release water vapor from the needles to the air. This release creates tension that pulls up a chain of water molecules, one at a time. The adjustments involved in this movement are reflected by the shrinking and swelling of a tree trunk. Measurement belts placed around trunks indicate that trees typically shrink in diameter during sunny summer days when the stomata are so many leaky faucets. The trunk then swells during the night as water is sucked from the soil by the tree roots. Most of this shrinking and swelling occurs within the bark, because even though bark is dead and designed to protect the tree, it remains flexible. The columns of water ascending the interior of a tree sometimes break, as David Haskell overheard with his ultrasonic sensor, but they are also sometimes restored, and life goes on. As a tree grows taller, however, maintaining the interior flow becomes more difficult because breakages occur more frequently. The ability to lift water thus likely limits the height of tree growth.

Trees must also grow thicker as they grow taller to keep from toppling under the force of even light winds. Some species augment their stability with buttress roots, but not spruce. Why grow tall? Access to sunlight drives some growth. Increased food and water storage likely also drive growth. Although the vagaries of existence can distort the orientation of its trunk, a tree will adjust to continue growing upward. If a spruce is tilted by wind or snow accumulation, for example, compression wood composed of more rigid, woody lignin forms on the lower side of the trunk and pushes the trunk upward, as revealed later in asymmetrical growth rings.

The spruce of this tale eventually grows to a height of 120 feet after two hundred years and then grows upward very little with increasing age. The spruce is tall and slender, and from a distance its needles appear to hang down like long fur on an animal. During cone season, the immature, striking pale magenta or purple cones stand upright on the branches. As the cones mature later in summer, they relax to hang slightly downward and take on a honey-brown hue. Autumnal hoarfrosts highlight individual needles with long, delicate ice crystals that disappear with the rising sun. After winter storms, each branch sags slightly under its weight of snow.

Cones grown and released, snows falling and melting, summer thunderstorms followed by clear sunsets. As time passes, the spruce grows within through the complexity of its mycorrhizal networks and its endophytic communities, and outside through the colonization of its crown by other fungi and lichens.

Mature spruce growing along the bank of a creek in northern Colorado. This photo, taken in late August, shows the cones clustered at the top of each tree.

The spruce is now part of an old-growth stand. Forest is considered old growth if most of the trees in a stand exceed two hundred years in age. Old-growth forests have not only large trees but also large numbers of standing dead trees known as snags. Abundant downed wood creates a forest floor with peaks of fallen logs next to valleys where snow settles more gently, creating buried air pockets in which a pine marten or spruce grouse can take refuge from winter's cold temperatures. The closed canopy of the old-growth forest has its own arboreal peaks and valleys that allow limited sunlight to reach the forest floor.

Studying a subalpine forest dominated by Engelmann spruce and subalpine fir in northern Colorado, Mary Arthur and Timothy Fahey found that the living, aboveground portions of the trees constitute only 30 percent of the total mass of living or dead organisms. A small percentage of this biomass is in the roots (6 percent), a little more is on the forest floor in the form of litter and duff (16 percent), 4 percent is in snags, and just over 12 percent is held in downed, dead wood. Thirty percent of the forest biomass is in the soil. In other words, the soil holds as much hidden biomass as do the trunks, branches, and needles of the conifers. If this is broken down into the nitrogen required by all plants, 26 percent of the nitrogen present in the forest stand is in living, aboveground portions of the trees, while 56 percent of the nitrogen is on the forest floor, and just under 10 percent is belowground. When we enter a forest, we tend to look upward to the trunks and canopy, but most of the action is at our feet.

Clearly, the dead plant material on the forest floor forms a rich reservoir of nutrients for living trees and other organisms. This reservoir persists through time. The average time that litter and duff remain on the forest floor in a Colorado subalpine forest before decomposing is just over thirty years. The distinction between litter and duff reflects the gradual decomposition of sloughed plant parts. Litter consists of distinct, readily identifiable bits of plants—needles, cones, scales of bark. Duff is the amorphous residue that is still composed of plants, rather than mineral soil, although individual bits are no longer easily identifiable. The long residence time of litter and duff provides more opportunity for microbes and fungi to gradually break down the dead plant parts. Litter and duff capture raindrops and melting snow, allowing water to percolate into the soil and keep it moist despite drying winds and sunlight. The layer of dead plant bits also helps protect the underlying soil during wildfires.

Nitrogen can remain on the floor of the old-growth forest for almost a century, and phosphorus for sixty-five years. These residence times are longer than those in younger forests because the progressive accumulation of litter and duff is like a steadily growing bank account on which living organisms can draw for nutrients without depleting the capital.

Other organisms begin to grow on the mature tree, as well as the endophytic bacteria in the needles and the ectomycorrhizal fungi in the roots. Although Engelmann spruces in the subalpine forests of Colorado are not festooned with long strands of lichen or blotchy with bromeliads clinging to their trunks, they do have canopy epiphytes. Epiphytes grow on the surface of a tree and derive their moisture and nutrients from precipitation and the air. Individual epiphyte species have preferences. Some like the trunk, others the branches, the lower or upper part of the tree, and so forth. These organisms include lichens, a word that derives from the Greek verb *leikhēn*, meaning "to lick" or "to eat around oneself." Tree lichens do eat around themselves, but in the process they can help their host trees eat, too.

Lichen consists of algae or cyanobacteria living among filaments of multiple species of fungi. The fungi do well because they get carbohydrates manufactured during photosynthesis by the algae or cyanobacteria. The algae and bacteria do well because they are protected by the fungal filaments, which also gather moisture and nutrients. A lichen is thus a community in itself.

Each tree hosts a community of lichen species that reflects the particular tree. Different tree species have different lichen communities, in part because of the rate at which the tree bark sloughs off—lichens don't like a shaky foundation any more than people do. The environment around the tree also influences lichen communities. Trees growing in a clump tend to have more lichens per branch than solitary trees. Lichens in the upper canopy get more sunlight, so lichen diversity and biomass are usually higher in the upper canopy. On the other hand, lichens growing in the upper canopy dry more quickly following precipitation.

Drying is critical because lichens can take up minerals that provide nutrients only when their tissue is saturated. They can assimilate minerals from precipitation, from the surface on which they grow, or from particles deposited on them. Whatever the source of the minerals, water is required. Water is not present for very long in the canopy, so lichens have evolved the ability to rapidly bind nutrients from solution. Lichen tissue is rich in sites where chemicals can be exchanged between water and lichen, and this helps lichens grab more minerals while wet. The pH of the environment influences the lichen's ability to take up minerals, and the acidic conditions of most conifer bark exclude many species of lichens. Numerous lichen species can survive on conifer bark, however. One study in the Colorado Rockies found forty-six species of lichens, two species of moss, and one species of fungus growing on Douglas-fir and fir trees alone, providing a window into the potential diversity of an entire forest.

As a tree ages, more lichen species can take up residence. An older tree has more diverse microhabitats to support different types and has been available for lichen colonization for a longer time. Older people take comfort in the thought that experience can bring wisdom. If trees were sentient, perhaps the older ones might pride themselves on how the diversity of their lichens improves their ability to obtain nutrients.

In the process of keeping themselves alive, the canopy epiphytes and the bacterial endophytes in the forest help keep the trees alive by fixing nitrogen. These arboreal communities also change the chemistry of rain and melting snow filtering down from the upper tree branches. Water falling and dripping through the canopy picks up nutrients such as calcium, magnesium, sodium, and potassium, as well as dissolved organic carbon. Some of the newly dissolved material comes from nutrients that the canopy organisms leach from the trees. Some comes from windblown dust that settles onto the treetops. Whatever the source, differences in the chemistry of water falling from the sky and water reaching the forest floor reveal the canopy as far more than a physical structure of branches and needles. The living community of the canopy reacts with everything brought by the winds and thus influences what wind and water can deliver to the forest floor.

The spruce grows and diversifies, taking on a weight of lichens on its branches and bark, bacteria in its needles, and fungi in its roots, providing nurturing shade for spruce seedlings and understory herbaceous plants, and perhaps communicating with neighboring trees through the wood-wide web.

Life in the Forest

The maturing spruce lives within a community whose members have their residences, their daily commutes and work, and their leisure and play. As in any human city, patterns of activity change through the day and with the seasons. Permanent residents and visitors partition themselves into neighborhoods that are zoned vertically but also reflect qualities largely invisible to human eyes.

In the days after the winter solstice, mountain chickadees are the most visible and readily heard residents of the spruce's community each morning. Small gray-and-white birds with a raccoon-like black eye mask, the chickadees call with a forceful *dee-dee-dee* that reverberates through the canopy year-round as the birds seek seeds in winter and insects during summer. Chickadees are the heroes for spruce and pine trees when a beetle outbreak occurs. Their rapid, darting motions require a steady stream of food: a half-ounce bird probably needs about ten calories a day to survive. Burgeoning beetle populations provide a chickadee banquet, and the birds gorge. In winter, the conifers repay the favor as the chickadees strip and eat seeds from cones.

Brown creepers also live in the forest year-round, but they are the introverts among birds, too busy with the business of living to continually announce their presence. The bird's mottled brown, white, and tan back and head blend so well with a tree's trunk that a creeper resembles a moving piece of bark as it walks a spiral path up the trunk. Creepers provide a grooming service for a tree. The bird starts near the ground and systematically proceeds up the tree to nearly the top, then moves up along the next tree, gleaning insects as it moves. Creepers remain close to the bark even when nesting, for they manage to build a nest between the trunk and a loose piece of bark on a large tree.

Creepers moving up a trunk may pass red-breasted nuthatches moving down the same trunk on the same errand. The black-and-white-striped head, cinnamon

breast, and gray back of the nuthatch are more easily noticed than the covert coloring of the creeper. These avian extroverts follow a zigzagging path down the trunk,
using the large claw on the one backward-pointing toe on each foot to maintain a
firm grip on the tree bark. This is summer behavior, though. In winter, they rely
on conifer seeds, some of which they cache during summer. Like a chickadee, the
small nuthatch is a bundle of aggressive energy. Despite its relatively long, stout bill,
a nuthatch seems far too diminutive to excavate a nesting cavity, but these birds are
among the few nonwoodpeckers that do gouge their own cavities from solid wood.
The nuthatch then uses an ingenious strategy to fend off interlopers. The bird plas-
ters the rim of its cavity nest inside and outside with resin globules and itself avoids
the sticky resin by diving directly through the cavity hole.

A splash of red among the white snow and dark canopy reveals the presence of
a red crossbill, a finch that appears to have a defective beak. The crossed tips of the
beak are quite functional, however, allowing the bird to pry into tightly closed conifer cones and extract the unreleased seeds. Unlike chickadees, creepers, nuthatches,
and other birds that change their seasonal diet from summer insects to winter seeds,
crossbills live on seeds alone, even feeding them to their nestlings.

Pine siskins also live in the forest year-round. Siskins resemble sparrows with
yellow highlights, but they spend most of their time feeding on seeds high in the
canopy and are hard to see from the forest floor. Similar to the chickadees feasting
on insects, pine siskins can temporarily store a mass of seeds up to 10 percent of
their body weight in their esophagus. Imagine a 140-pound woman eating fourteen
pounds of meat at a sitting.

Of all the birds moving within the canopy during daylight hours in winter, the
chickadees are the most likely to be seen and heard. Their mammalian counterparts
in visibility are the chickarees, or pine squirrels. Green cones harvested during summer and autumn and stored in caches to prevent the release of the seeds now provide a winter larder for the squirrels.

Far quieter and slower moving than the squirrels, porcupines are also active in
the forest canopy during winter. Although porcupines prefer to eat the phloem of
ponderosa pines, they will also consume the cambium, buds, and needles of other
conifers, including Engelmann spruce. Just as nitrogen is a critical, hard-to-obtain
nutrient for plants, it is also a critical nutrient for porcupines. The bark, twigs, and
conifer needles of the animal's winter diet are poor in nitrogen, so porcupines lose
weight throughout the winter in a sort of slow-motion starvation until summer
brings better food.

Down on the forest floor, the crisscrossing tracks of birds, rodents, hares, and larger animals record daytime and nighttime wanderings. Least chipmunks venture out during the day from their dens beneath tree roots and fallen logs. The swift little animals spent the summer hoarding scattered seeds in pits concealed beneath downed logs. This supply fuels their metabolism through the winter, much of which the chipmunks spend in a deep sleep snug in their burrow.

Dusky grouse, chicken-sized birds whose brown-and-gray-speckled bodies blend so well into the shadows of the forest floor when there is no snow, remain active by day during winter. The birds feed extensively on spruce buds and needles and use small spruce trees for protective cover and winter roosting sites.

Mule deer, elk, moose, and bighorn sheep can all pass through stands of Engelmann spruce when seeking refuge from storms or extreme cold. They are transients, though. The elk and moose travel long distances but seek out tender willows, aspen, and river birch along streams. The bighorns prefer the rocky terrain of the peaks to the dense forest of the valley floors, in part to avoid the mountain lions that also move through the forest.

As darkness falls on the spruce stand in winter, different residents wake and start the nightly search for food. Among the smallest are the southern red-backed voles, short-tailed rodents that tunnel through the snow during winter. Just about anything serves as vole food—seeds, nuts, insects, snails, berries, roots, and the mycorrhizal fungi in the roots. The voles are particularly effective at dispersing mycorrhizal fungal spores through their feces, helping to widen the web through the woods. They also rely on winter food caches of plant parts gleaned and stored during summer.

Voles seek out portions of the forest floor with abundant downed wood in which they can take shelter, but the metabolism of predators active throughout the winter is just as demanding as that of the voles, and many of the rodents fall prey to coyotes, foxes, boreal owls, ermine, and pine martens. Incredible as it might seem to human ears, many of these predators can hear the soft sounds of a vole tunneling beneath deep snow, even when noisy, strong winds send the snow crystals slaloming down snowdrifts. Coyotes and foxes take a characteristic stance, head cocked first to one side and then the other so that their acute hearing can pinpoint a vole's location. Sure of its prey, the larger animal backs slightly and then arcs upward into the air, driving its front paws and head down through the snow in a pounce that captures the unfortunate rodent.

Having spent the daylight hours roosting quietly on a branch and coughing up a daily pellet of indigestible bones and fur, boreal owls are ready to hunt again as darkness returns. Sitting on a hunting perch, the small owl (less than a foot tall) with a big head and the characteristic intense owl stare waits for rodents and squirrels before swooping down to attack with its talons. The boreal owl's much larger relative, the great horned owl, also hunts rodents by night, but the larger owls can also eat hares and porcupines.

The snowshoe hare's brown summer coat has changed to a camouflage white for winter, and it seeks daytime refuge beneath the widely spreading branches of conifers close to the ground. Emerging at dusk from a shallow depression it has scraped out under covering branches, a hare starts to feed on the needles, twigs, and bark from conifer trees that keep the animal alive during winter. Hares are silent and cautious, with good reason. Even their ability to dance in winter by taking long leaps without sinking into the powdery snow does not always save them from death from the sky when an owl descends on broad, silent wings.

Bobcats, coyotes, pine martens, and other predators of the ground also kill hares. Pine martens choose old-growth stands like the one in which the Engelmann spruce grows, where cavities and logs provide them with den sites. During winter, the mature, dominant individuals claim resting sites associated with downed wood beneath the snowpack, where the animals can warm the air space with their body heat and rest for longer periods before returning to the hunt. The behavior of martens and many other animals reveals how fallen and decaying trees, which may seem like unsightly or cumbersome obstacles to people, function analogously to the infrastructure of a human city, creating housing and pathways for travel.

Eventually, summer comes to the Northern Hemisphere. Glorious summer—season of light, warmth, and babies in the old-growth forest. Those who have slept the winter away emerge hungry. Black bears wake up ready to eat just about anything, from a vulnerable newborn fawn to the shoots and buds of trees or the larvae and adults of bees and ants.

The quiet songbirds of winter become vocal as they attract mates and stake out territories. Summer migrants arrive. Hermit thrushes return to feed on insects, and their lovely whistling calls once again echo through the canopy. Williamson's sapsuckers, beautiful black-and-white woodpeckers with a red chin patch and yellow belly, arrive to nest in the spruce. The sapsuckers mine tree trunks, drilling rings of shallow holes around a tree and then eating the sap. The seed eaters of winter switch to eating insects, combing the furrows of tree bark and picking tiny bodies off the needles and branches or plucking insects in midair.

Birds from the diminutive nuthatch to large woodpeckers tattoo the tree trunks, in both senses of the word, sending out a rhythmic pounding and permanently marking the trunks. Small excavations lead to insects for food; larger excavations produce cavity nests, preferably in spruce snags a foot or larger in diameter. Boreal owls seek out older cavity nests abandoned by woodpeckers. So do pine squirrels, which start steadily clipping and eating the newly growing spruce twigs and buds, taking time out only to chase one another or loudly announce to the entire forest the presence of a human visitor.

The passing seasons have their rhythm, punctuated by storms and the changing population of plants and animals as the forest ages. Just as a human life grows rich with accumulated experience and memories, the spruce tree gathers an increasingly rich load of other creatures that live on its bounty.

Senescence and Death

Senescence derives from the Latin *senex*, "old." Senescence can be described as the process of deterioration with age, the fate of every living organism fortunate to live long enough to achieve natural deterioration. Senescence comes to an aging tree as the tree outgrows its ability to obtain sufficient resources to stay alive. As self-maintenance gradually loses ground, the tree becomes increasingly susceptible to the

The riparian zone of a stream in Colorado following an intense wildfire in 2020. The smaller burned stems in the foreground are willows and the trees in the rest of the photo are young to mature conifers.

many sources of mortality lying in wait: wildfire, windstorms, lightning, disease, and insects.

Wildfire is critical to the survival of many tree species, but not Engelmann spruce. Even low-intensity fires can kill spruces, which do not have the thick, fire-resistant bark of the mature ponderosa pines that live at lower, fire-prone elevations in the Colorado Rockies. Individual spruces or small clusters of trees may escape burning if they grow in very wet locations where fire does not spread well, but the common occurrence of even-aged spruce stands suggests that many of the trees germinate after a fire has killed their predecessors.

Blowdowns also claim many trees where the Engelmann spruce grows. Every winter the winds take down some trees and weaken others. Standing trees with the crown still attached can be so twisted and torn partway up the trunk that the tree dies the following summer. Other trees sway and creak, the torque of wind in the canopy progressively pulling at even the largest roots that have fingered down into fractured bedrock. If the entire tree comes down, chunks of bedrock come up with the roots. When a large tree with wide-spreading branches goes down, it can carry with it branches or trunks of neighboring trees. Sometimes, a treetop is sheared off

A blowdown along North St. Vrain Creek that occurred during the winter of 2011–2012. Several years after the blowdown, the fallen and partly fallen trees form a tangle of wood beneath which it is hard to see one of the secondary channels of the creek.

by winds, only to be caught and held, suspended above the ground, by the branches of adjacent trees. Many of the trees lying thick on the ground in the old-growth spruce forest were taken down by wind.

An Engelmann spruce is subject to other slings and arrows of outrageous fortune. A tree may be struck and killed by lightning or be the ignition point for a wildfire. Lightning is the danger of late summer when thunderstorms brew up most days over the high peaks and then sweep down the slopes and valleys. Fungal diseases such as snow mold fungus attack tree roots, stems, and branches. The most common diseases are those caused by wood-rotting fungi that decrease wood volume and make living trees or snags more susceptible to windthrow and windbreak. These diseases receive particularly unattractive names—root rot, butt rot, trunk rot, or spruce broom rust, which causes deformation of the trunk and spike tops (forked crowns) in living trees.

The spruce of this tale does not die by fire, wind, lightning, or disease, however, but by beetle. After 450 years of life, the massive tree is taken down by a very small insect.

Whole families of beetle species make their living parasitizing trees. Most of these are native species, rather than introduced tree killers such as Dutch elm disease or emerald ash borer, which can largely kill off a particular tree species across an entire continent. One native insect that affects Engelmann spruce is the western spruce budworm. Although the budworms are always present, every thirty to forty years or so, budworm populations increase to outbreak levels. During these outbreaks, the budworms cause extensive defoliation, reduce the growth of some trees, and kill others, changing what grows where, and how fast, within affected forest stands. Budworm larvae feed on cones, seeds, vegetative and reproductive tree buds, and new needles. When the current year's foliage is consumed, the budworms move on to older foliage. Engelmann spruce is less susceptible to spruce budworms than some other types of conifers, but the trees do suffer from beetle outbreaks.

The great insect killer of Engelmanns, however, is the spruce beetle, which may be as important as wildfire by killing entire stands of spruce trees. Most of the time, the beetles maintain low population levels. Under these conditions, spruce beetles may benefit overall forest health by feeding on stressed or fallen trees and thereby providing food and habitat for wildlife. But then, episodically, beetle populations erupt and kill healthy, vigorous trees across huge swaths of country. In the 1990s, such an outbreak killed three million mature spruce trees in Utah. During the six major outbreaks of spruce beetles that have occurred in the Southern Rockies since the mid-1800s, the beetles have in places killed up to 99 percent of the mature, moderate to large spruce trees in a forest. Engelmanns continue to be widespread in the American West because the beetles do not attack small, young spruces. The beetles seem to prefer larger trees because of the greater nutritional quality of these trees and their thicker bark, in which the beetles breed. This selectivity allows Engelmann spruce to continue to exist and of course allows young trees to grow up into beetle homes.

Female spruce beetles locate a suitable host tree, bore through the bark, and send out invitations for a housewarming. By releasing pheromones that waft through the air, the newly housed female attracts large numbers of male and female beetles. A healthy tree possesses defenses lethal to bark beetles. Resin flow can create a physical barrier to beetle entry. The tree can muster chemicals toxic to beetles. So, the first beetle calls in her friends to create a density of attack sufficient to kill the tree. The swarm of beetles focuses on the northern side of the trunk, where cooler temperatures and a little more moisture in the inner bark tissue beneath the shaded trunk favor the hatching and growth of young beetles.

Spruce beetles mate within the tree, and within a week the female deposits eggs in a gallery that she excavates in the phloem. The first part of the gallery has a slight crook, but the remainder goes straight up the phloem, with ventilation holes at intervals along its length. As the gallery lengthens, more of the initially excavated portion is packed with larval poop known as frass. Adult beetles are about a quarter of an inch long—the size of a grain of rice—yet they can excavate a gallery that may be just over two inches long, or a whopping (for a small beetle) nine inches long. This beetle skyrise quickly hosts an entire community because of the wide array of microorganisms that the beetles carry with them.

To say that the beetle excavates a gallery and then throws a party might be an understatement. Spruce beetles carry at least eight species of mites and six species of nematodes, as well as fungi and bacteria. Some of the fungi and bacteria might facilitate the beetle's digestion of the tree's tissues, the synthesis of beetle pheromones, or the depletion of the tree's defenses. For phloem-eating species such as spruce beetles, whose food is nutritionally poor, fungi may provide an alternative source of nutrients. Some of the bacteria might inhibit species of fungi that injure the spruce beetles. Whatever benefits they provide, a lot of microbes ride along with the beetles and take up residence in the tree.

The swarm of organisms entering the spruce tree through beetle boring calls to mind Jonathan Swift's lines written in 1733 as part of "On Poetry, a Rhapsody":

> So, naturalists observe, a flea
> Hath smaller fleas that on him prey;
> And these have smaller still to bite 'em;
> And so proceed, ad infinitum.

One species of fungus is found on nearly all adult spruce beetles. This blue-stain fungus infects the tree's phloem and sapwood, which responds by creating solid, waxy compounds known as sterols. Insects need sterols to support molting and reproduction. In effect, fungal hitchhikers on the beetles cause the tree to create chemicals that the beetles require. Meanwhile, the drying of damaged vascular tissue in the host tree disrupts the tree's ability to conduct water from the roots to the needles. The daily interruption of water flow in the xylem that David Haskell described as sounds of mounting distress must rise to shrieks of agony in a beetle-infested tree.

Adult beetles commonly attack host trees during June and July. Nearly all the resulting beetle eggs hatch by mid-October and the larvae reach the next phase of their development. The larvae overwinter in the gallery and then resume development in the spring. About a year after the initial attack, the larvae become pupae and transform into adults. The adults pass a second winter within the tree and then emerge the following summer to attack new tree hosts. This is the general schedule, although times vary depending on factors such as air temperature during each year.

Most of the new attacks occur along the lower part of a tree's trunk and are limited to about ten per square foot at breast height. The number of tiny beetles needed to take down a huge spruce varies with the density of the attacks and the surface area of the tree's bark. A lot of beetles are needed to kill a large tree, but more beetles are also drawn to the largest trees.

The beetles do not have everything their own way, however, and the spruce has allies in its battle against the beetles. Predaceous beetles and flies and parasitic wasps kill substantial numbers of spruce beetles. Chickarees eat spruce beetle larvae, especially when conifer seeds are not abundant.

A spruce's best friends in the fight against the beetles, however, are woodpeckers. Other birds including gray-headed juncos, mountain bluebirds, and mountain chickadees eat beetles during the flight and dispersal of the insects, but woodpeckers are the great consumers of spruce beetles. Depending on the beetle population density and larval size, woodpeckers can kill anywhere from 20 to 98 percent of the little wood munchers. The key species in this regard are northern three-toed, hairy, and downy woodpeckers. The northern three-toed are the most effective consumers because they feed exclusively on tree trunks and primarily on the trunks of freshly attacked trees rather than old snags, as well as congregating in beetle-infested tree stands. Hairy woodpeckers also feed on tree trunks but take beetles from old snags as well as recently attacked trees. Downy woodpeckers feed mainly on the branches of infested trees and therefore are less effective than the other woodpecker species in reducing beetle numbers. All these woodpeck-

A pine squirrel among fallen cones and needles.

ers nest in cavities excavated mostly in snags. The snags that are likely to be more abundant in an old-growth forest than in a younger forest stand are like army barracks, housing the woodpecker-soldiers so important in a spruce tree's fight against beetles.

If the tree of this tale were sentient, it might ask, Why now? Why me? Outbreaks of spruce beetles in some part of the Southern Rockies seem to occur about every twenty years. Seasonal weather patterns, blowdowns, and wildfires can create favorable conditions in a particular forest stand. The presence and susceptibility of host trees govern beetle population dynamics. Newly fallen, stressed, and weakened trees can foster outbreaks. Beetles can have a field day when drought limits the defenses of trees over a wide area. More local outbreaks may occur in areas of blowdowns or wildfire. Ultimately, however, beetles are always present in a forest. They survive in relatively small numbers in weakened trees, snags killed by root disease, and downed logs, waiting for a group of trees to be killed or become sufficiently stressed to host a beetle outbreak. As warming climate increases tree-stressing droughts in the western United States, spruce beetles may find life increasingly good.

After an outbreak kills mature spruces, the young surviving spruces and neighboring subalpine firs can experience a growth spurt. A few trees die in blowdowns each year and then a few hundred die in a microburst. A local beetle population boom kills a small stand of trees elsewhere in the forest and a decade of drought allows the beetles to spread across miles of forest. A lightning strike starts a fire that burns large holes into the blanket of forest across an entire watershed. The forest mosaic of differently aged trees and mixtures of spruce, fir, and other species is a story map of the history of disturbances and tree responses over hundreds of years.

Life after Death I: Snag

Once the swarming spruce beetles and their associated fungi choke the spruce tree to death, readily visible changes occur on the tree. The needles turn a reddish brown and, by the second summer following the infestation, fall from the tree. With them fall the endophytes and canopy epiphytes of the living tree. The finer branches break off quickly, but the base of a larger branch can persist for years as the trunk remains standing as a snag. During the first two decades after the beetle infestation, about half the snags may fall to the forest floor as the trunk breaks or wind uproots the tree. A few snags remain upright for decades. The wood of the tree dries out and, in the chill climate of the Colorado subalpine, decays very slowly. Thus the dead tree enters its next phase of existence, in which the snag continues to host numerous living creatures.

The most charismatic occupants of the snag are the cavity-nesting birds. Primary cavity nesters—woodpeckers, flickers, sapsuckers—start the process by excavating the initial holes in the tree. These birds can find even small patches of decayed wood on an otherwise sound snag. Decay in trees is either heart rot or sap rot. In either form, fungi break down the woody tissues of the tree. The fungi that create heart rot enter the living tree through the roots, through wounds in the trunk caused by fire or by accidents that expose heartwood, and through broken branches or tops. Most living trees have some heart rot. After the tree dies, the heart rot continues to move vertically within the trunk as well as into the sapwood to create sap rot. This sap rot causes wood decay from the outer layers of the trunk inward.

Woodpeckers are the house flippers of the forest. They create a nesting cavity, use it one year, and then move on. The longer a snag persists, the greater the density of cavities it may host along its length. Once the woodpeckers have built the neighborhood, secondary cavity nesters join the community of the snag. Swallows, bluebirds, and eastern screech-owls, and boreal, flammulated, and other owls, as well as kestrels, flycatchers, wrens, chickadees, and creepers all use existing cavities. Most of them feed primarily on insects during summer, helping to limit insect damage to living trees in the forest. This is why dead trees can help keep the living trees in a forest healthy. Trees that reach a ripe old age before dying and then form broken-topped snags greater than twelve inches in diameter attract the most bird use, but snags provide birds with far more than nesting sites.

Snags can be the concert stages of the forest bird community. Beyond the obvious—singing—snags provide excellent drumming sites. Woodpeckers, for example, do not have a distinctive song. Instead, they communicate by rapidly pecking something that resonates, creating a pattern of sound that can seriously

A snag in the early phases of decay (*left*) and in the late phase when only the lower portion of the tree remains standing (*right*).

distract a human householder when the resonant object is a chimney or an air vent on a roof.

Snags serve as bird restaurants, too. Insect-eating birds probe the slowly decaying wood for tiny moving bodies. Seed eaters may cache seeds in the snag. Owls perch on remaining branches while scanning the forest floor for the next meal. A snag makes a very nice plucking post on which a raptor can dismember its prey, or an anvil where birds such as thrushes smash snail shells against the wood to extract the soft flesh.

Snags provide lookouts as well as landing and roosting sites. Even with all the surrounding activity, snags also serve as so-called loafing sites that are not connected with feeding or breeding—typically, places for preening and resting.

In addition to providing a restaurant for birds, snags become a restaurant that serves up birds. Predators including black bears, raccoons, and pine martens can extract eggs or nestlings from a cavity nest, or simply rip apart the whole cavity to get at their prey. Sometimes the prey is much smaller than eggs or nestlings, however. Black bears, in particular, can pulverize significant sections of a snag that have been colonized by carpenter ants or termites. That's one way to seriously hasten the processes of decay.

Snags serve as initial nesting sites for carpenter ants, but the ants seek old-growth trees for permanent nests. Winged young ants leave the nest in early spring, dispersing in all directions to mate. Males die shortly after mating, but young, mated females can replace old queens in established colonies or establish a new colony in a small cavity of a snag or fallen tree.

The new queen constructs a brood cell by enclosing the cavity, then breaks off her wings and begins to lay eggs that will hatch in just over a week. She feeds the newly hatched larvae on secretions from her salivary glands, even while fasting herself. The larvae develop, spin cocoons, pupate, and emerge as adults, all within a month after hatching. The first brood takes over the work of the colony, cutting parallel, concentric galleries longitudinally through wood soft from decay and enlarging the galleries as the colony grows. All this new construction generates a lot of waste, because the ants do not eat the wood they excavate. Instead, they cut openings from the gallery to the outside and cast the excavated wood bits into space, creating accumulations of sawdust-sized fragments below access holes. Worker ants secure food such as caterpillars and honeydew secreted by aphids and bring the food into the colony through these access holes. Other workers feed the queen and care for the eggs she lays and the resulting larvae. Like a nanny carrying or feeding a baby, these nurse ants shuttle larvae and pupae to the most favorable places within a colony, as well as helping the young adults emerge from their cocoons.

With the addition of bacteria, fungi, and diverse invertebrates to its tissues, the snag contains substantial living biomass, albeit in a different form than when the tree was alive. Nutrients carried in on rainfall and snowmelt also accumulate on the snag.

So the spruce snag continues to provide valuable habitat that supports a wide array of organisms and influences the availability of food and habitat in its vicinity.

For seventy years, storms come and go and the snag sways in the wind, creaking and groaning under the force of the gusts. The outer surface of the wood weathers to streaked hues of tan, orange, and gray, and the texture of the wood becomes more apparent. Then, inevitably, comes a gust too strong. The snag breaks a few feet from the ground and the remaining branches shatter as the trunk hits the forest floor. Once again, the community of the tree is reset as the cavity nesters move elsewhere and creatures of the forest floor move into the newly available wood.

Life after Death II: Logjam

The impact of falling snaps off the highest part of the trunk, which falls into North St. Vrain Creek. The piece of wood is only four feet long and four inches in diameter, but the snag falls in autumn and the flow in the creek is too low to move even such a small piece. The wood rests on one bank and a cobble protruding above the water surface. Overnight temperatures start to dip well below freezing and ice forms in the creek. First comes frazil ice in the form of delicately interlocked, slender crystals at the water surface. Then the frazil ice thickens downward to the stream bed and forms anchor ice around the cobbles in the bed. Over a period of days, a skin of ice seals over the water surface and then grows thicker as snow begins to accumulate on it. By early winter, the creek is hidden beneath a gently undulating surface of snow. Water continues to flow beneath the ice, but a portion of the broken snag is frozen into the ice and the wood remains stationary.

Spring brings lengthening days and warmer air, although the narrow, shaded river valley remains colder than the adjacent uplands. In late May, the snow cover along the creek finally melts out along with the ice, and the water surface rises with snowmelt coming from across the drainage basin. The piece of spruce wood is lifted and carried swiftly downstream, mostly slipping smoothly by obstacles along its path, but occasionally smacking into a protruding boulder or a larger piece of wood. The piece travels only a few hundred feet downstream before it collides with the upstream side of a logjam. The force of the water flowing against the jam keeps the spruce piece pinned in place, even while other pieces of wood and smaller bits of needles, cones, and sand and gravel pile up against it. By the time the snowmelt peak flow recedes, the piece of spruce is firmly wedged into a logjam that extends across the creek. Each succeeding night the flow rises with the remaining snowmelt and the logjam expands and dilates, like a body inhaling a deep breath, only to contract and sink slightly as flows decline during the day. The repeated expansions release some of the smaller wood pieces in the jam, but the spruce piece remains in place.

A logjam in North St. Vrain Creek. Here, the broad log at left is effectively creating a partial barrier that traps other, smaller wood pieces moving downstream. The pool at right is much deeper than other parts of the creek.

The jam creates a sizable backwater even during low flow. Aquatic mosses colonize rocks and pieces of wood in the pool. Green strands of filamentous algae sway in the current.

As the current slows coming into this backwater, sand and silt, pine needles, and small twigs settle to the stream bed. This plant detritus is an important part of the base of the food web in this small forest stream that is too shaded by adjacent trees to support a dense growth of photosynthetic aquatic plants. Microbial communities known as a biofilm colonize the organic detritus in the pool, forming a thin, slimy layer over everything on the stream bed. The aquatic larvae of mayflies, stoneflies, and caddisflies come to feed on both the decaying bits of plants and the biofilm. Trout seek out the pool, too. Protruding portions of the logjam provide cover under which the fish can hide from predators. Slower flow along the edges of the pool allows the fish to rest in a spot from which they can easily dart out to snag a passing aquatic insect in the nearby swifter current or an unwary terrestrial insect that flies too close to the water surface. Fish biologists examining the stomach contents of the brook trout that are most common along this portion of North St. Vrain Creek find that the fish eat mostly ants, bees, and wasps. One overachieving brook trout that

An underwater view of the backwater immediately upstream from a logjam. Pieces of variously sized wood lie on the bed and project upward, creating overhead cover for fish. The aquatic plants in the foreground grow more luxuriantly in the slower current of the backwater, and sand (the pale portion of the stream bed in the middle ground) accumulates in the backwater. The logjam is at right, and light reflects off the underside of the water surface.

was scooped from the water during a fish census, however, had a vole halfway into its mouth. This would be like a human swallowing an entire chicken headfirst.

The logjam partly blocks flow moving down the creek and forces some of the water into the stream bed. The water flows a short distance through the porous and permeable sediment of the hyporheic zone, from the Greek words *hypo*, "below," and *rheos*, "flow." This underground flow consists of water that moves from the creek into the subsurface below the channel and the floodplain and then returns to the creek downstream. Known as the river's liver, the hyporheic zone hosts its own microbial and aquatic insect communities. The microbes, in particular, can change the stream-water chemistry by removing nutrients. The sojourn in the cool depths also helps keep stream waters cooler.

The logjam also blocks much of the surface flow in the stream during snowmelt, causing the water level in the creek to rise. As the stream water spills over the channel banks and across the floodplain, some of it infiltrates the ground and maintains wet soil that supports different plant species from those on the adjacent, drier slopes. Some of the water flowing down and across the floodplain concentrates in slight depressions. There the force of the concentrated water begins to erode a new channel that parallels the main channel for a couple of hundred feet before rejoining the main channel downstream. This secondary channel has shallower, slower, warm-

A portion of North St. Vrain Creek in which multiple logs have wedged between trees on the valley floor at left, creating a broad backwater pool during early summer snowmelt and multiple smaller channels that branch and rejoin downstream from the logjam.

er flow than the main channel, and although the smaller channel goes dry late in the summer, it provides habitat for smaller fish and different aquatic insects during snowmelt.

The logjam is like a customs agent extracting some of the riches from the swiftly flowing water of the creek. A creek moving downstream without interruption is duty-free. By forcing some of the water to move more slowly across the floodplain and through the hyporheic zone and by trapping some of the plant detritus carried along by the flow, the logjam extracts a tax in water, nutrients, organic matter, and fine sediment from the creek. This tax creates ideal habitat for a greater variety of microbes, plants, insects, and fish within and beneath the creek. These organisms in turn support bats, songbirds, raptors, spiders, and other creatures of the surrounding forest.

The piece of spruce within the logjam creating all these effects undergoes repeated wetting and drying as flow in the creek rises and falls with the seasons. When other wood around the spruce piece moves or is detached by the flow, the spruce piece is eventually exposed on the upstream side of the jam.

Three years after joining the jam, the spruce piece is battered and broken by cobbles moving along the stream bed during a year of high snowmelt. The fragments of wood move downstream to the next channel-spanning jam, where they are trapped in the backwater and decomposed by aquatic fungi that colonize the wood pieces. Aquatic insects then further fragment the wood pieces by feeding on the microbial fungi, a process that stream ecologists have likened to chewing through the wood to get at the peanut butter of the nutritious fungi within the wood tissue. Tiny, rounded bits of wood produced by breakage, abrasion, and insect fragmentation form much of the visible organic detritus that collects upstream of the logjam.

Eventually, most of the piece of spruce in the stream is broken down into its constituent nutrients, which go into the tissues of other living organisms or into solution in the stream water. The wood that may make the stream look messy has given and given, directly and indirectly creating habitat and food for a broad array of organisms that live within the creek as well as those that feed on fish or on insects emerging from the creek.

Life after Death III: Coarse Woody Debris

The fall of the rest of the snag onto the forest floor marks the start of the next phase of the tree's deterioration on land. Forest ecologists call such large pieces of downed wood coarse woody debris. The spruce falls on the floodplain perpendicular to the flow of North St. Vrain Creek. When the creek overflows its banks with snowmelt in early summer, the large, stable, fallen trunk collects sediment on its up-flow side. Plants, including spruce seedlings, germinate on the freshly deposited sediment and help fix the newly forming soil in place. Invertebrates and small vertebrates start to burrow into and mix the soil, as well as adding the nutritional enrichment of their feces.

The force of falling causes the trunk to crack and split, allowing it to dry slightly. Wood-boring beetle larvae, ants, and termites tunnel through the remaining bark and the wood, further weakening the wood and inoculating the downed log with microbes living on or within the insects. Openings created by the insects expose the wood to colonization by other microbes and small invertebrates. Wood-rotting fungi create larger zones of weakness, especially between annual rings. Imagine the tiniest line of weakness possible, and some organism has evolved to exploit that infinitesimal space for its own habitat and food.

The fallen tree begins to decay more quickly. Branches and the narrower top of the trunk decay most rapidly because of the greater proportion of sapwood to heartwood. Burrowing insects and plant roots fragment the wood, creating more new surfaces at which fungi and microbes can enter. Over the succeeding eight hundred years, the entire tree gradually becomes an amorphous, homogeneous mass.

A portion of the forest in which abundant fallen trees create coarse woody debris on the forest floor. The downed trees in the foreground have lost their bark and branches.

En route to this state, the log loses more than half its volume as bark and sapwood slough off and are consumed and fragmented by plants and animals. Sloughed bark and wood accumulate in a mulch surrounding the log. The log grows narrower more rapidly than it grows shorter, but fragmentation does reduce the length. The decaying wood becomes more like a sponge as it grows moister and less dense. The larger the log, the more plant litter it accumulates on its surface and the more nutrient-rich moisture it intercepts from water falling through the canopy. Fungi inhabiting the wood absorb nutrients and enrich the decomposing wood. Nitrogen-fixing bacteria colonize the fallen tree. Through various mechanisms, the fallen tree gains minerals and nitrogen while losing its woody cellulose tissue.

Myriad organisms facilitate these changes. Wood can be broken down by consumption and digestion by insects and attacked by enzymes released from microbes. Insects are faster but also help speed attacks by microbes. Wood-boring beetles and termites chew through the wood fibers, creating physical cavities that jump-start access to the wood by other organisms. Among the wood borers are predaceous species such as checkered beetles, which prey on bark beetles. Beetle and termite boring increases surface area and the extent of internal spaces, as well as introducing microbes such as intestinal microorganisms expelled in the insects' feces. Newly enlarged internal spaces within the wood can then be occupied by bacteria and fungi, as well as plant roots, wood-tunneling mites, collembolans, amphibians, and small mammals.

Collembolans are tiny, wingless insects that jump using a springlike appendage on the abdomen and hence are also known as springtails. Along with mites, collembolans can use tunnels made by other insects to penetrate deep into the decaying wood, where they graze on bacteria, fungi, and decaying vegetation. Multiple species of both mites and collembolans colonize the tree with time. When the mites and other invertebrates die, some types of mycorrhizal fungal spores can use their empty exoskeletons as incubators. Other, predaceous mites move in and eat collembolans, arthropod eggs, small roundworms, and sometimes each other. As mites go, the predaceous species are long legged and fast, with strong mouthparts for capturing and chewing their prey.

All of this sounds like something from science fiction: First come the beetle and termite miners, boring a maze of tiny tunnels through the interior of the wood. Bacteria and fungi grow along the tunnels. Collembolan and mite grazers follow their food sources into the tunnels. Fungi grow on the bodies of those who die in the tunnels. Predators sweep through the tunnels at unpredictable intervals, seeking live prey.

Bacteria and fungi are smaller than the wood fibers, and once they gain entrance to the fallen tree, they slowly dissolve and enter the wood cells. Most plants that grow on the rotting wood require mycorrhizal fungi to survive. Although fewer species of mycorrhizal fungi grow on wood than in soil, the appropriate fungi species arrive as spores on the wind, as hitchhikers on insects or small mammals, or as passengers in raindrops. Like trees growing on soil that collaborate with mycorrhizal fungi, plants growing on the fallen tree develop an association with fungi in the decaying tree tissue.

Mites and beetles eat the mycorrhizal fungi. Other types of mites, spiders, pseudoscorpions (which are relatives of spiders), centipedes, and salamanders come to eat the smaller invertebrates. Earthworms, millipedes, isopods, and earwigs move in to feast on dead plant and animal material and animal feces. In essence, insects, bacteria, and fungi start making the fallen tree sufficiently porous to allow flows of plants and animals, air, water, and nutrients between the downed tree and its surroundings. Once the insects, bacteria, and fungi set the dining table, a host of other creatures come to feed. As David Haskell put it, "Rot is a detonation of possibility."

Red-backed voles exemplify interactions within fallen trees. The voles depend on downed wood for cover, as well as eat fungi and lichens, with a preference for mycorrhizal truffles that fruit in decaying wood (these are cousins of the truffles famous among epicures). The voles in turn disperse the fungal spores to the rotten wood in which the fungus thrives. Instead of a vicious circle, this is a circle of support: the vole needs the truffle for food; the truffle needs the vole for spore dispersal; the truffle needs the mycorrhizal tree host for energy; and the tree provides the downed wood that shelters the vole from predators.

Other small mammals are predators. Shrews eat many of the invertebrates found in fallen trees. A shrew looks like a mouse that is long at both ends, although shrews are not rodents; they are in the taxonomic category known as Eulipotyphla. Rodents are in Rodentia, and although we sometimes use the epithet "rodent" as an insult, "Eulipotyphla" is even less flattering: its Greek roots signify "truly fat" and "blind."

The shrew's total length of four to five inches is more than half tail. A long, pointed nose completes the other end. In between is a voracious stomach. Although weighing only about two-tenths of an ounce, a shrew must consume somewhere between half and twice its own body weight in food every day to maintain the metabolic rate needed to keep its little body warm. Shrew food is insects and their larvae, earthworms, spiders, and snails, all of which can be found in rotting logs. Shrews have poor vision, but what is there to see inside a rotting log? There is a great deal to smell, and shrews use their acute senses of smell and hearing to find their tiny prey. As for defenses, shrews are venomous. Grooves in their teeth carry very potent venom into predators unfortunate enough to be bitten.

As it is for many animals, winter is a time of hardship for shrews. Although a shrew can become torpid in the winter, it undergoes an amazing winter metamorphosis in which its bones, skull, and internal organs shrink in size as the animal loses a third to half of its body weight. When fully awake during the warmer months, shrews are fiercely territorial, coming together only to mate. Such coming together is pretty frequent, however, given that females can have up to ten litters a year during the warmer months. Babies have a gestation period of two weeks to a month, but a female can become pregnant within a day or so of giving birth, nursing one litter until the next one is born. There is no downtime for female shrews except during winter when they nearly starve to death. Life in the fast lane, indeed, at least for a year or so. Then it ends.

Each portion of the fallen tree supports a characteristic community adapted to specific circumstances. Proteins concentrate in the inner bark and cambium, which are also more readily digested than sapwood, and these areas support different species of microbes, fungi, and invertebrates than the heartwood. And, just as the tree species composing a forest may go through successive changes following a disturbance, so the inhabitants of a fallen tree change with time. The earliest invaders are opportunistic scavengers: fungi and bacteria that, along with insects, exploit the readily available carbohydrates in cambium, phloem, and sapwood. These early scavengers prepare the ground for their successors, including fungi that are better able to decompose the decay-resistant cellulose and lignin in the sapwood.

In the last stages of decay, the visible remains of the fallen tree are little cubic chunks of brown, rotted heartwood. The spongy wood separates into angular chunks that may be held together only by lichens, mosses, liverworts, and the roots of herbaceous and woody plants. Now the log may become a nurse tree with a line of seedlings and saplings growing along its length.

At the end, the fallen tree is a long, low, amorphous mound covered with litter and duff. New plants no longer establish on the mound because of the intense competition from roots already growing there. Only lignins, the wood compounds most resistant to decay, remain. Consequently, few decomposer organisms can live on the mound, which is dominated by mycorrhizal fungi. The moisture content remains high, providing a reservoir for living organisms during summer drought.

A later stage of wood decay, with the heartwood separated into small cubes, and mosses and fungi growing on the upper and lower portions of the log visible in this photograph.

The nutrients contained within the tree have cycled between organisms many times. Nitrogen incorporated into the wood-cell structure as the tree grew has been extracted from the wood during decomposition by fungi and bacteria and incorporated into their own cellular structures. Mites, collembolans, and beetle larvae feed on fungal and bacterial tissues enriched in nitrogen from digestion of wood. Vertebrates from red-backed voles to mule deer obtain some of their nitrogen from decaying trees by feeding on the fungal fruiting bodies of truffles and mushrooms. As it decomposes, the fallen tree returns its nitrogen to the forest ecosystem.

Having formed as a product of soil and photosynthetically captured carbon, the tree ultimately becomes soil, releasing its carbon to the atmosphere through decomposition and returning other nutrients to the soil and the larger ecosystem. This helps make the valley-floor soil along North St. Vrain Creek particularly fertile and rich in carbon.

Decaying logs are only one of the contributors to the soil. Freeze-thaw cycles of water gradually wedge apart the underlying granite bedrock, and the organic acids released by plants and soil organisms change the chemistry of the rock. Despite these attacks on the bedrock, the cold, dry climate of the mountains cannot produce thick, rich soil. Glaciers and wind help. Abrasion by boulders frozen into glacial ice pulverized some of the bedrock and supplied the silt and clay particles known as rock flour. However, wind has been the primary source of fine sediment to soils in the Colorado Rockies since the retreat of the glaciers fifteen thousand years ago. Silt and clay blow in from the deserts of the southwestern United States, and even across the Pacific Ocean from Asia's Gobi Desert. Moving down into the rocky, sandy soil with percolating rainwater and snow, these fine sediments help the soil retain moisture.

This is the endless sequence of the seasons, the years, and the millennia: Bedrock cracks and weathers. Wind drops silt and clay onto the hillslopes, and water moving downslope carries the sediment onto the valley floor. The creek overflows its banks and deposits more sediment across the floodplain. The channel moves sideways around a logjam that has collected organic matter in its backwater pool. The jam and filled pool become part of the floodplain soil. Plants drop leaves, needles, branches, and cones that decay and are consumed. Entire trees fall to the forest floor and return the nutrients that they sequestered during their lifetime to the reservoir of the forest soil.

The Engelmann spruce plays its part in this continuing drama of creating and enriching the soil that supports the ecosystem of the valley floor. Ashes to ashes, dust to dust, and rot to soil and new growth.

The Second Tree: Lowlands

A Western Redcedar in the Queets River Valley of Washington

Western redcedar (*Thuja plicata*) is a tree of damp, shaded regions, able to thrive in swamps and along stream banks, and to grow under dense shade. From the forest floor, the trunks of mature trees are most noticeable. Solid, straight, slightly tapering columns covered in furrowed, reddish-brown bark rise up and up, with nary a branch in sight. Only by leaning backward and gazing up can you see the feathery leaves shaped like ferns on branches high in the canopy.

Western redcedar along a stream bank, ready to fall in and join the logjam at left if bank erosion undercuts the tree.

The scientific names reflect the appearance and scent of the tree. *Thuja* comes from the Greek *thuia*, "fragrant." *Plicata* comes from the Latin *plicare*, "braided," which describes the pattern of the tree's small leaves.

Redcedar is one of the most widespread trees in the Pacific Northwest region of North America, typically growing with Douglas-fir and western hemlock. These trees could just as well be called not-cedar, not-fir, and not-hemlock. Redcedar is a native in the cypress family and its common name is spelled as one word, rather than "red cedar," in recognition that the tree is actually not a member of the genus

Cedrus, and therefore not a true cedar. The common name has changed through time, but the first Europeans to encounter the tree, including Meriwether Lewis, referred to it as a cedar. Douglas-fir is in the pine family, not a true fir (again, the hyphenated name is a clue). And hemlock's common name derives from a similarity in the scent of the tree's crushed foliage to that of the unrelated poison hemlock plant. That's why scientists prefer Latin names.

Redcedar groves now extend from sea level to more than seven thousand feet in elevation, following lowlands in bands parallel to the Pacific coast. Studies of DNA in *Thuja* suggest that the genus evolved in high-latitude areas of North America some sixty million years ago. In a migration the reverse of that assumed to have originally peopled the Americas, *Thuja* subsequently expanded into eastern Asia across the Bering Land Bridge. *Thuja plicata* appears to have waited out the Pleistocene glaciation in a refugium south of the ice before following the retreating glaciers northward along multiple river valleys. This is one of the advantages of releasing enormous numbers of seeds from each plant. Some of those seeds may reach newly exposed terrain suitable for germination, allowing the plant species to expand its geographic range.

The Queets River valley is well suited to a tree that prefers abundant moisture and low light. The river flows from mountain glaciers directly to the Pacific Ocean. North St. Vrain Creek flows over ancient granite that has been repeatedly lifted up by forces in Earth's interior, cracked, and weathered. The Queets flows over geological youngsters.

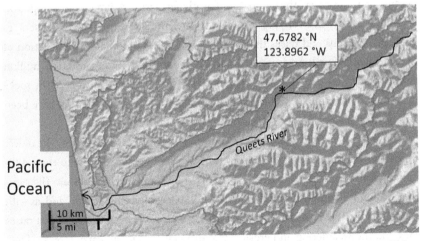

Map of the location of western redcedar within the lower drainage of the Queets River, which flows westward to the Pacific Ocean.

Earth's surface is divided into tectonic plates that float about like (very heavy) rafts on the planet's underlying molten layers. Plates that form the continents tend to be composed of lighter rocks, whereas those that underlie the oceans consist of heavy basalt. The plates continually jostle one another along their edges, and the jostling margins crumple up into mountain ranges or erupt in volcanoes. The massive Pacific Plate and a few smaller plates push against the western edge of the North American Plate, giving rise to spectacular peaks like the Cascade Volcanoes. These volcanoes are fed by the melting of the Pacific Plate as its leading edge is forced down into the planet's interior in a process geologists call subduction. As the subducting oceanic plate melts, some of the molten material rises back toward the surface and erupts in volcanoes.

Off the mouth of the Queets, the meeting of plates occurs between the giant North American Plate and a smaller one known as the Juan de Fuca Plate after the nearby Strait of Juan de Fuca between Vancouver Island and the Olympic Peninsula. The original Juan was a Greek maritime pilot who served Philip II of Spain—Juan de Fuca is the Spanish spelling of his name—and he may or may not have first explored the eponymous strait. Regardless, his name is now well established in the region.

The Juan de Fuca Plate started to collide with the North American Plate about thirty-four million years ago. The great shaping of Earth's surface cumulatively moves slowly, although individual changes can be as abrupt as a fifteen-minute earthquake. Uplift of mountains along the line of this collision started about twelve million years ago as the subducting slab of oceanic rock began to underplate the western edge of North America. "Underplating" is a nice name for a messy, violent process. As the oceanic slab goes down, the bedrock and overlying marine sediments are scraped off and mashed onto the overlying continental plate. The stacking of successive scrapes gradually thickens and raises the overlying rocks into mountains. The portion of Mount Olympus still present started to be underplated about seventeen million years ago and now sits eighteen miles above the subducting slab. More of the rocks forming the mountain have been raised through time, but those rocks have been removed by the erosion of glaciers and rivers.

The entire Olympic Peninsula is a young addition to North America. The oldest exposed rocks date to only about fifty million years ago, in contrast to the 1,420-million-year-old rocks underlying North St. Vrain Creek in the Rockies. The summit of Mount Olympus currently stands at 7,980 feet above the Pacific, and, as with any mountain, that height reflects the ongoing seesaw between the uplift that raises rock and the weathering and erosion that dismantle rock and carry it away down river valleys.

From the bright heights of white ice and snow and pale gray rock, the streams of glacial meltwater cascade down quickly into narrow, forested valleys. Joining to form the Queets, the waters enter the broad-floored, steep-sided glacial trough of the lower river. Remnants of past glory linger in several small glaciers on the southwestern side of Mount Olympus that now supply the river with glacial meltwater. Superimposed on the glacial melt are contributions from rainstorms, especially when spring rain falls on melting snow.

The Olympic Mountains rise steeply inland from the coast, creating a wall that catches moisture moving eastward. Abundant rainfall supports dense forests of Sitka spruce and not-cedar, not-fir, and not-hemlock throughout the watershed. Streams and rivers create slightly sunnier openings in the otherwise closed forest canopy, and bigleaf maple, red alder, and other deciduous trees crowd the stream banks. Conifers cover slightly higher, drier portions of the floodplain back from the channel.

Wildfire is not as frequently a hazard for trees in the coastal lowlands of the Olympic Peninsula as it is in the Southern Rockies. Individual studies have estimated a wildfire recurrence interval of 1,100 years for the coastal forests, for example, and more than 4,000 years for western Olympic National Park. Landslides and avalanches, however, periodically strip trees from the hillsides, and floods rip up trees along the valley floors. Winter rains can sometimes swell the river's flow from its average yearly level of 4,350 cubic feet per second to a flood of more than 100,000 cubic feet per second. Such floods rearrange the channels that wind back and forth across the valley floor. The big floods also pile up enormous logjams.

Tracks of a River in the Forest

The lower portion of the Queets River meanders broadly across the valley floor. A meandering river takes and gives back: each bend migrates sideways through time as the outer part of the bend erodes and the inner portion collects sediment to build a point bar. As the bend continues to migrate outward, plants colonize the point bar and the bar merges into the floodplain. Most of this bend migration occurs during floods, which also cause more abrupt change when the channel cuts across the neck of a particularly sinuous bend, or the entire channel abruptly shifts to the other side of the valley. This restlessness on the part of the river creates a twisting ribbon of differently aged stands and species of floodplain trees that are immediately apparent as varying shades of green and different textures of foliage in aerial photographs. The river leaves a track of its progress through time in the ages and types of trees growing on the valley floor.

In this aerial view of the lower Queets River course, recently inundated gravel bars appear as pale gray, stands of younger deciduous trees appear as intermediate hues of gray, and older conifers are darker gray. The river flows from right to left, and just over three miles of channel are shown here.

Changes in soil and vegetation as the river moves across the floodplain follow a consistent sequence through time. This is the recipe for a floodplain soil: First, the channel deposits the sand of the point bar over the cobbles and boulders of the main channel. The closely growing seedlings and saplings of pioneer trees such as willow and alder, as well as downed large wood deposited by the river, can slow the water flowing over the surface, allowing more of the sediment suspended in the water to settle out. Sediment continues to accumulate rapidly during the first decade or two as the channel gradually moves farther away, but more of the sediment is silt and clay rather than sand and gravel. The fine sediments increase the soil's ability to retain water and nutrients.

Second, the young trees that have colonized the former point bar shed leaf litter and enrich the soil with organic matter. Growth may be slow for a few years, however, because the soil does not have many nutrients. A critical third phase occurs once the red alders growing on the old bar acquire rhizosphere friends in the form of ectomycorrhizal and bacterial communities. Now the alder can start fixing nitrogen in the soil and trees can grow faster. In the last phase, chemical weathering of the newly deposited sediment releases phosphorus in a form available to plants, as well as elements such as potassium, sodium, and calcium. In addition to being nutrients, these elements help keep the soil from becoming too acidic and limiting plant growth.

If this floodplain soil recipe is like a cake, the Pacific Ocean provides the frosting. Out at sea, the wind whips the waves to whitecaps—alliteration at its best. The white of the caps is air, and when the air bubbles burst or the wind tears drops of water from the wave crests, aerosols form. An aerosol (a term far more familiar to most people now than it was before the COVID-19 pandemic) consists of microscopic particles dispersed in air. Aerosols torn by the wind from the turbulent surface of the ocean are mainly simple salt, or sodium chloride, but can also include potassium, calcium, magnesium, and other elements that were dissolved in the seawater. When carried onshore, these elements act as nutrients for plants. Aerosols from the Pacific can be carried up to thirty miles inland before they drop to the ground and help fertilize floodplain soils.

The aerosols are largely invisible. A far more apparent source of marine nutrients to floodplain soils are the bodies of large, dying fish. Salmon returning upstream to spawn carry within their bodies a wealth of ocean-derived nutrients. Spawning complete, the dead and decaying fish release the nitrogen, carbon, and phosphorus that they have acquired during a lifetime of feeding in the ocean. This, too, enriches the floodplain soil.

Although the soil grows more fertile with time, other stresses can limit the survival of the plants on the former point bar. Elk wander through and browse on the young forest. They selectively eat the growth tips of the plants, and too many animals or too many return trips can stunt the woody vegetation. Beavers choose succulent stems of willow growing on the point bar, too, but the beavers gnaw through the base of the stem and the willow responds with a new shoot. During the largest flows, turbulent water carries gravel particles that roll and bounce along the bar, abrading the saplings. Water can submerge the old point bar for days to weeks, and this too the saplings must survive. Despite these stresses, a dense thicket of willow and alder gradually covers the point bar.

Birds come to the thicket. A pair of olive-sided flycatchers build a nest back from the young deciduous forest, in the nearby conifers, but not too far from the water and its abundant flying insects. During the breeding and nesting season, the air over the river is lively with this pair living up to their name, capturing insects from flies to dragonflies on the wing. Their nest is a small cup, perhaps three inches across, built on a foundation of twigs and lined with grasses and lichens. Until the fledglings leave the nest, this little cup is the flycatchers' world. The pair aggressively defend a territory that may exceed a hundred acres, and they are capable of knocking a squirrel off a nearby branch and chasing it out of the neighborhood.

Hutton's vireos nest in the forest interior, too, building a cup suspended from a forked branch and hidden by overhanging lichen. These pale gray birds with white and a hint of yellowish green in their coloring blend well into the shifting light and shadows of the deciduous forest on the point bar. Unlike the flycatchers with their aerial acrobatics, the vireos move slowly and deliberately through the foliage, plucking insects and spiders.

Within about thirty years, willows mostly disappear from the site and alders become the dominant trees. *Frankia*, a filamentous bacterium that converts atmospheric nitrogen into a form available to plants, colonizes the alder roots. The alders grow faster, and nutrient-poor sediments rapidly become nutrient-rich soil. Hardwood decay fungi are also present, and within forty to seventy years the alders begin to die, opening the canopy and allowing sunlight to reach the forest floor. The rich soils, partial shade, and greater protection from floods allow shade-tolerant conifers such as Sitka spruce and Douglas-fir to colonize the site.

While the forest remains mostly deciduous, a distinct suite of birds uses the old point bar. Black-throated gray warblers and chestnut-backed chickadees pluck insects from trees and shrubs in deciduous forest, where warbling vireos eat mainly caterpillars, pupae, and adult moths and butterflies. Hairy woodpeckers and diminutive Hammond's flycatchers breed in sites where deciduous and coniferous trees intermingle.

The plumage of the flycatchers is a pale gray hood and cape over black-and-white wings and a pale yellowish-green breast. This muted coloring hides a fiery temperament. While territories and mates are being sorted out in spring, males can fight so fiercely that they lock together in midair and flutter all the way to the ground before shaking themselves apart. Their hunting is more deliberate. Perching silently, a Hammond's will scan the surroundings before flying quickly upward to capture an insect in flight or hovering briefly to glean an insect from the vegetation. Returning to the perch to eat, the flycatcher sometimes removes the wings or whacks the insect against a branch. Perhaps all that wing fluttering is unsettling to the flycatcher as the butterfly or moth goes down its throat.

Western spotted skunks live in the deciduous forest, too, occupying dens created by rodents and eating everything from berries and insects to small rodents and birds and their eggs. Larger striped skunks like the mixed woodlands of deciduous and coniferous trees. Cats large and small—the cougar and bobcat—are generalists that range through diverse types of forest, the cougar preying on deer and elk and the bobcat on rabbits and hares.

As the conifers mature, an understory of maples, western redcedar, and western hemlock develops. Now most nitrogen comes from free-living bacteria in the soil and decaying downed wood. Bird life diversifies. Pairs of lemon-yellow Wilson's warblers take the apparently risky approach of building their nest in a small depression on the ground at the base of a sapling or a downed log. Seemingly always in motion, the adults forage through the understory for larval insects, spiders, beetles, and caterpillars. The male, his black cap looking like a tiny toupee, interrupts his hunting for brief snatches of song. The warblers are joined by more subtle-hued Pacific-slope flycatchers. These flycatchers have distinctive white eye-rings. The birds venture out from their cavity nests in the forest to hunt insects in the interior foliage of trees or large shrubs. Round-bodied, short-tailed wrens also find nesting cavities and feed themselves and their nestlings on insects. Hermit warblers, with strikingly yellow faces above a gray, black, and white body, pick insects from branches and foliage in the canopy.

Given the avian feeding frenzy and the many gaping little mouths to stuff with insects, it is perhaps remarkable that any invertebrates survive in the forest. Certainly, the birds help limit the damage that insects do to vulnerable young plants, so this is a good site for the western redcedar of this tale to begin its life.

Germination and Seedling

The cones of a western redcedar are about as large as the tip of an adult human's finger, a size that seems ludicrously small for such an enormous tree. Each cone produces only three to six small seeds, but each tree has so many cones that from one hundred thousand to one million seeds can be dropped on each acre of ground. Seeds fall from the cones during October and November. These seeds are not carried as far by the wind as the seeds of adjacent trees such as western hemlock and Sitka spruce, but the area within three hundred feet of a mature redcedar is well covered with potential future redcedars.

Although most seeds escape consumption by rodents and birds, many seeds simply do not germinate. Western redcedars hedge their reproductive bets by also using vegetative reproduction. Aboveground portions of a redcedar stem can grow roots while still attached to the parent plant and then detach as an independent plant. Fallen branches can also take root, and branches can grow from fallen trees. The resulting "veglings" can have a long and healthy life, but they do not create the genetic diversity that represents the ultimate hedging of bets against some future catastrophe that could wipe out a whole population of genetically identical clones.

Successful seeds germinate above the ground, sending a protoroot down from the surface. Germination can occur at any season but must take place during the first year. Western redcedar seeds in old-growth stands do particularly well in rotten wood that is in contact with the soil: the new seedlings germinate from the bodies of their ancestors. Although western redcedars can grow on soils low in nutrients, having enough nitrogen, calcium, and water allows seeds to germinate and grow more rapidly. Drought, sunlight, and high soil temperatures are the enemies, so partial to full shade is important. Young redcedars can sunburn severely. Frost is also a danger.

The tree of this tale germinates in a patch of forest rich with tree diversity. The neighbors include Sitka spruce, which can live for seven hundred years and grow to heights of more than two hundred feet. The conical crown of a younger spruce gradually occupies less of the tree's overall height as lower branches break off with aging—a bit like the receding hairline on an aging human head. Western hemlock trees, with their short needles and pendulous branch tips that give the trees a feathered appearance, have grown up in the shade of other trees that the hemlocks eventually replace. The trunks of the conifers are so broad, gently tapering, and lacking branches at the lower levels that the trunks resemble columns and inspire the often-repeated image of a cathedral forest.

Bigleaf maples, with leaves up to a foot across, are shorter than the spruces and hemlocks and grow dispersed under the canopy of the conifers. Red alders grow taller than any other alder species in North America, but they still top out below the big conifers, as do the black cottonwood trees, which have a spindly trunk lacking branches that stretches up and up to a branched, leafy tuft at the very top. The flexi-

ble stems of vine maples resemble a large shrub. When I view these deciduous trees from the forest floor on a sunny day, the dense moss and lichens covering the trunk and inner branches create a dark, furry core surrounded by a vibrantly green halo of sunlit leaves. In autumn, the dying leaves of the deciduous trees create arboreal flames of yellow and red among the more somberly hued conifers.

The undercanopy is colorful with tall shrubs that produce flowers and berries: red flowers and juicy-looking, reddish-orange berries with a ruff of pink hairs for salmonberry; white flowers and red fruit for thimbleberry; extravagant masses of pinkish-white flowers on Pacific rhododendron;

Sunlight filters through the canopy of an Olympic Peninsula forest, highlighting bracken ferns in the foreground, snags at left, and the feathery foliage of the canopy.

hanging white bell flowers and dark blue berries on salal; and pinkish-white blooms and scarlet berries on red huckleberry. Densely growing stands of two-to-three-foot-tall bracken ferns cover hundreds of square feet. Oxalis forms patches of emerald green on the forest floor amid the ferns and mosses that cover downed wood, rocks, and soil like a thick carpet. And then there is Devil's club, with its apt Latin species name *horridus*. The flexible stem and both

Blossoms and foliage of Pacific rhododendron, wet after a rainstorm.

the top and bottom of each huge leaf are covered in spines. Even the flowers, tiny and greenish white on a large stalk, are not particularly attractive.

Apart from the spines of the salmonberry and Devil's club, this forest is soft with moss underfoot and layers of leaves filtering whatever sunlight penetrates from the often-cloudy sky. Rain falls throughout the autumn, winter, and spring, adding up to a total of nearly twelve feet of precipitation. Plants crowd atop one another. Long streams of epiphytic mosses and lichens hang down from tree branches. Moss and lichen blur the outlines of tree trunks and branches. Sounds are muted, and the world is mostly green.

The redcedar seedling expands into the surroundings. Lateral shoots grow faster than the terminal shoot, and the growth of roots and associations with mycorrhizal fungi develop as in the Engelmann spruce seedling. Redcedars differ from spruces in having extensive roots. One accounting found that redcedars created only 17 percent of the volume of trees in a forest but grew 82 percent of the root length in that forest. These are relatively fine, shallow roots rather than deep taproots. Redcedar roots cannot penetrate the dense, clay-rich soils on which the trees commonly grow. Many of the roots may even lie within a thick duff layer rather than in the underlying mineral soil. Whether in mineral soil or duff, redcedar roots develop mycorrhizae as primitive fungi grow into the roots. Fungi colonizing the outer layer of the roots form a microscopic network of filaments strung with little sacs.

Despite the dangers of direct sunlight, the seedling is of course photosynthetic and grows upward toward the sun at a rate of about one and a half to two feet per

Moss covers many surfaces in a temperate rainforest, from hanging branches to downed wood and boulders.

year during the first five years. This is comparable to growth rates of neighboring Douglas-fir, western hemlock, and Sitka spruce seedlings. After that, the race toward the sun becomes uneven. Douglas-firs and western hemlocks grow taller more rapidly, but the redcedars also accelerate their upward growth during their second decade. By age five, the dominant redcedar individuals are already taller than those redcedars that will never reach the top of the forest canopy. And, although shade is necessary, individual trees in a dense stand grow more slowly than those in a slightly more open setting.

Beyond the competition from neighbors, redcedar seedlings and saplings can suffer from intensive browsing by black-tailed deer or elk. During the fall rut, deer stags can thrash and damage redcedar saplings with their antlers. Rodents can also browse and damage seedlings and saplings. The tree of this tale survives the gamut of physical damage and hungry mouths and continues to grow upward.

Sapling

Once they reach ten years of age, western redcedars begin to produce cones every other year. Male and female cones grow on different branches of the same tree. The scientific term for individual plants that include male and female reproductive organs is "monoecious," derived from Greek roots meaning "single house" (mónos, "alone," and oikos, "house"). Tiny orange-and-brown male cones grow on the tips of the leaves along the lower branches. Larger, more elaborately shaped female cones grow closer to the treetop.

The sapling continues to grow upward at the rate of just over one and a half feet each year, adding perhaps half an inch of radial growth to the trunk every year. Because the redcedar grows under a closed canopy, it develops a tall, straight single stem rather than the multiple tops that can form in open canopies.

Not all the neighbors fare so well. In spring, black bears can girdle and kill trees to feed on the newly forming phloem. A single foraging bear can peel bark from up to seventy trees per day. So-called mountain beavers (although rodents, they are no relation to real beavers) and porcupines can also girdle tree trunks near the ground. Complete girdling all the way around the trunk kills a tree. Partial girdling weakens it by providing access for insects and disease.

Tree growth can also be depressed by a severe freeze, such as one that occurred in November 1955 across the Pacific Northwest. The cold damaged cambium and phloem on parts of exposed trees and left a record of crooked stems at the point of the freeze and compartmentalized rot in tips of branches below this part of the stem. Redcedar growth can also be suppressed by too much shade, leaving trees that are two hundred years old but only three inches in diameter and twenty-five feet in height. Redcedars can survive suppression because tall, dominant trees in a stand can indirectly support continued growth of the roots and lower trunks of suppressed trees by enhancing the abundance and diversity of ectomycorrhizal fungi in the forest soil. As in the Colorado subalpine forest, the wood-wide web supports the weaker members of the tree community. The sapling of this tale is not girdled, depressed, or suppressed, however, and continues growing toward its eventual place in the upper canopy.

Maturity

The mature western redcedar is both impressively large and beautiful. The tree rises two hundred feet from a trunk ten feet in diameter. The trunk tapers upward, covered in fibrous, reddish-brown bark that can be peeled in thin layers. In this closed-canopy forest, only the upper branches remain on the trunk. Lower branches die and eventually break off. Flat sprays of tiny, green, scalelike leaves grow from the living branches. When crushed, these leaves release an aroma reminiscent of sharpening a wooden pencil. Because lack of moisture is not typically a problem on the Olympic Peninsula, the leaves of the redcedar are not protected from water loss by a thick layer of cutin and wax, as are the needles of the Engelmann spruce.

A close view of redcedar leaves, here lying on a sandbar beside the river, showing the braided appearance from which the leaves derive their Latin species name.

As the stand surrounding the redcedar becomes old growth, the physical characteristics of the forest environment grow increasingly complex and rich. This is far from a plantation forest of evenly aged, evenly spaced trees. The decaying skeletons of snags stand like punctuation marks among the living trees. Some of the rain falling on the canopy may never reach the forest floor because the dense, multilayered canopy intercepts the raindrops, but the lower canopy remains more humid because the dense layers of greenery above protect it from sunlight and wind. These cool, moist conditions slow the decomposition of downed wood, which can persist for many centuries and lies strewn thickly across the forest floor. Wood makes up more than half the total mass of organic material on the forest floor, even though the downed trees can be difficult to discern beneath a mantle of litter, duff, and understory plants. Western redcedars contribute more than their fair share to the downed wood, thanks to their large trunks and resistance to decay. This decaying wood forms an important reser-

A fallen log in an advanced stage of decay, covered in moss and supporting seedlings. The log blends into the forest floor so well that it is hard to see, but in this photograph the log is oriented from the center foreground toward the center rear.

voir of nutrients. About half the nitrogen and 60 percent of the phosphorus stored in the forest are in downed wood.

In a younger forest, the canopy is relatively simple, with a single layer at the top. As the forest ages, the mass of the canopy clumps into multiple layers of foliage with gaps, beneath which grow younger trees. More dead branches are present on trees, especially lower on the trunk. Branches large and small provide more diverse habitat than the uniformly sized branches of a young forest. Large branches are the heavy lifters, carrying a greater mass and species diversity of epiphytes and invertebrates. Because canopy fungi and bacteria live on branches and foliage, more diverse specific sites within the canopy support a more diverse community of fungi and bacteria.

The canopy fungi, bacteria, and epiphytes work for their host tree. Chemicals dissolved in precipitation increase in concentration as the water moves down through the layers of forest foliage. Picking up whatever is released by canopy organisms as it flows down tree trunks or drips from foliage, water reaching the forest floor is more acidic than the original rain or snow. Everything in the canopy—foliage, branches, and epiphytes—catches and keeps some of the matter and energy entering the canopy. The ability of canopy organisms to catch and keep varies with location in the canopy, but the entire community commonly catches about a quarter of the rain that falls and up to half of the snow.

The canopy is even more efficient at catching the nitrogen that is crucial to plant growth but present in low concentrations in rain and snow. When a vital nutrient is present only in dilute form, adaptations evolve to capture that nutrient. Nitrogen gas is present in the atmosphere, but plants cannot absorb it in that form. Bacteria can absorb nitrogen and release it as ammonium (a compound of nitrogen and hydrogen) or nitrate (nitrogen and oxygen). Only in the form of nitrate is nitrogen available to plants. The first fifteen feet of the upper canopy can catch more than 80 percent of the nitrogen deposited in the form of nitrate during the winter months, and both nitrate and ammonium during the summer. The canopy can even obtain nitrogen from water in fog or low-lying clouds.

What is actually capturing the nitrogen from the air? Everything—the foliage, epiphytic lichens and bryophytes, tree bark, and bacteria. Bryophytes are plants that reproduce by spores rather than via flowers and seeds. Bryophytes include mosses and liverworts, which are leafy plants commonly less than four inches long that look like flattened mosses. Bryophytes are commonly described as primitive plants because they do not have vascular tissue to transport water and nutrients (that is, the xylem and phloem of trees), and they lack true leaves, roots, and stems, not to mention flowers and fruits. Bryophytes nonetheless do quite well for themselves—just think about all the moss in moist environments. Cyanobacteria living in epiphytic bryophytes capture nitrogen at particularly high rates about a hundred feet above the forest floor. This rate is higher than nitrogen capture on the forest floor, despite the efforts of all the organisms in the rhizosphere.

The growth of many forests in temperate and high latitudes is limited by nitrogen availability. By capturing nitrogen, canopy organisms allow old-growth forest trees to continue to grow, even beyond eight hundred years of age. The small organisms obtaining the nitrogen—even the microscopic ones—are necessary to support the giant trees. Thanks in part to the nitrogen-grabbing epiphytes, temperate rain forests of the Pacific Northwest contain some of the tallest trees in the world and store some of largest amounts of organic matter of any type of forest. They also have the greatest density of carbon of any vegetation type in the world.

Carbon gets a lot of attention now because of the ability of carbon dioxide to trap the sun's warmth in the lower atmosphere. This is part of what keeps the planet livable for humans, but the burning of fossil fuels has pumped so much extra carbon dioxide into the air that we now face a rapidly heating atmosphere. In addition to trying to reduce carbon dioxide outputs, a lot of attention goes to trying to sequester carbon by "locking" it into ecosystems such as forests and wetlands or into soils. Old-growth forests remove carbon dioxide from the atmosphere and fix it into live woody tissue and slowly decomposing organic matter in plant litter and soil. The rate of carbon fixation varies with climate and nitrogen deposition, but the longer a forest persists, the greater the carbon accumulation.

The forest strains nitrogen from the passing air and stores carbon in its tissues. This is really a performance by the entire forest—the bacteria, fungi, epiphytes, and soil microbes—not just the trees. The more diverse and abundant the contributing organisms are, the greater the effectiveness of the forest in storing nitrogen and carbon. Older forests excel at this diversity and abundance.

The spatially heterogeneous old-growth forest canopy is like a city with a living space suited to every taste. Microenvironments with different levels of sunlight, humidity, temperature, and wind provide niches for a broad array of organisms. Prefer a protected environment that buffers changes in temperature and precipitation? The middle and lower portions of an old-growth canopy can provide that. Like sunlight and drier air? The upper canopy is a more changeable place on a daily basis than the lower canopy. The wind blows harder and both the daily heat and the nightly cold are greater. Residents must tolerate sunlight, drying, and low nutrients, so fewer fungi and bacteria live in the uppermost portion of the canopy.

How does the microbiota of fungi and bacteria get into the canopy? Many disperse via airborne propagules—bits of plants that, when detached from the parent plant, can land somewhere else and give rise to a new plant. The bits of willow stems that beavers partly chew and then drop into the current, for example, can land on a stream bank downstream and take root. Airborne propagules from fungi and bacteria are of course much smaller than chewed chunks of willow, but they operate in the same general way. Once established in the canopy, some are splashed by raindrops onto a new surface nearby. The structural details of the canopy influence this transport—the branches and foliage are like combs for the passing wind, catching fungi and bacterial propagules floating by, and the gaps between branches and foliage influence whether steadily falling raindrops can fling microscopic propagules from one surface to another. Combed or flung, a propagule lands on a surface where the microclimate will govern whether the tiny pioneer will survive. Conditions during which the propagules are sent into the world also influence survival; some fungal species release their spores during damp weather, others during dry weather.

Although the western redcedar is itself a living organism of great complexity, the tree is in a sense the structural foundation for all the other organisms that live on and within it. In addition to partitioning themselves among niches in the canopy and within wood, bark, and leaves, the fungi and bacteria inhabiting the redcedar create changes that influence the tree's growth and survival and provide habitat for other organisms. Fungi and bacteria decompose plant litter that collects on branches well above the ground, for example, and provide food for mites and other arthropods. Different species of wood-decaying fungi take up residence where the tree structure suits their needs, and a broken limb or wound on the trunk provides an entry point. Once these fungi establish in some portion of the canopy, they trigger sequential changes in which different microbial communities succeed each other through time within the decaying wood. The fungi promoting decay also provide food for invertebrates and vertebrates.

There is a lot of canopy in which fungi, bacteria, and other organisms can live. Forests on the floodplain of the Queets River can accumulate more than one hundred thousand cubic yards per acre of canopy volume, which is among the highest recorded on Earth. How to visualize one hundred thousand cubic yards? This is a volume that would cover an acre with a thickness of about sixty-two feet of material.

Canopy epiphytes in the expansive volume of this temperate rain forest are much more obvious and abundant than in the subalpine forest of the spruce in Colorado. Cat-tail moss coats branches in thick green mats. Forage lichens form pendulous drapes in shades of pale yellow, green, and brown. Cyanolichens that contain cyanobacteria, as well as other types of lichens, liverworts, and mosses, all crowd onto the redcedar.

Because epiphytes are not rooted in soil, they depend on atmospheric sources of water and inorganic nutrients. Even in a rain forest, rain does not always fall, so epiphytes have evolved the ability to dry and subsequently rehydrate. Bryophytes such as mosses and liverworts dominate in the dim light of the lower canopy. Cyanolichens such as *Lobaria oregana*, a lichen that resembles leaves of pale lettuce, prefer the midcanopy. Other lichens seek the bright light of the upper levels. The middle and upper thirds of the canopy each have about twice as many epiphyte species as the lower canopy, and the very upper portions of large trees have a unique community of lichens that uses the nutrients left by roosting and defecating birds. One creature's waste is another's food.

Epiphyte biomass slowly increases with forest age, and old-growth forests take the prize, supporting up to twice as many epiphyte species (one hundred or more) as a younger forest. When artistically limited people like me draw trees, uniform green blobs top the straight line of the trunk. Real trees possess differing degrees of structural complexity in the spacing and branching of their limbs. This complexity extends to the entire canopy as trees of different height grow closer or more wide-

ly spaced and their branches spread farther or cover a
narrower space around the
trunk. Individual trees of the
same species differ from one
another, and a forest composed of many tree species,
each with a general char-
acteristic shape, contains a
more diverse canopy, especially where snags bare of
needles and leaves interrupt
the foliage of the surrounding trees.

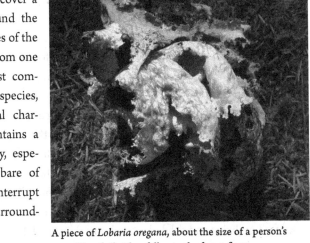

A piece of *Lobaria oregana,* about the size of a person's
spread hand, that has fallen to the forest floor.

With maturity comes
complexity and with com-
plexity comes weight. Mature conifers in the Pacific Northwest can hold 220 pounds
of epiphytes per tree, mostly in the foliage, but also on the branches and trunk. In the
Queets River floodplain, large individual trees can support more than 1,100 pounds
of bryophytes alone, plus another 1,000 pounds of ferns. To give this some perspective, an adult male grizzly bear in the salmon-rich environment of Alaska's southern
coast may weigh 1,100 pounds, and a grand piano weighs nearly 1,000 pounds. This
huge mass of other plants hanging on a big tree is not evenly distributed among all
the epiphyte species, however. In old-growth forests at low elevations, cyanolichens
in which blue-green algae are the photosynthesizers may form up to 80 percent of the
total lichen biomass.

Just as with every other form of life within and on trees, each species and group of
canopy epiphytes has its preferred location. Forage lichens that hang from branches
like long green tree-hair can dominate the upper, middle, and outer portions of the
tree crown. These lichens do indeed provide forage for animals from flying squirrels
to mule deer to people. Lower and inner portions of the tree crown may have more
diverse epiphytes.

Epiphytes, along with trees, continually shed dead plant material. Canopy soils
can form where this litter accumulates—on large branches, under and around epiphytes, or where decades of epiphyte growth and death form a mat of decaying organic material. These soils perched high above the ground are formed mainly from
dead and decaying moss and lichens and are like peat perched in the canopy. The

aerial soils can be a challenging environment in which to live, however. Although these soils can retain more water than mineral soil in the ground, they also dry out more during periods with no rain or snow. And the canopy soils, lacking the insulation of a ground soil, have greater fluctuations in temperature. Canopy soils have lower levels of carbon and nitrogen than soils at the forest floor, but they can derive nutrients from the foliage of the host tree and from precipitation and so support abundant invertebrates.

Just as the epiphytes partition themselves among different portions of a tree and different tree species, the invertebrates that live in the epiphytes also select their homes based on food source and microclimate. Comparisons of western redcedar and neighboring Douglas-fir, grand fir, and western hemlock reveal distinct species and community organization among canopy arthropods living in each tree species. Several types of mites, for example, live only on western redcedar. Tiny oribatid mites feed on living and dead plant and fungal material, lichens, and carrion. Plant litter falling onto branches high in the canopy and on the forest floor is rich in these mites. When scientists took the time to search, they identified fifty-seven species of mites in canopy and ground litterfall, with different mite species in the canopy and on the ground, in different epiphytes, and on different tree species. On western redcedar, foliose lichens that resemble a pale lettuce leaf support particularly rich mite communities. These mites can account for more than half the microarthropods in canopy soils on western redcedar. Patterns of oribatid mite species in dead bits of plants falling from the canopy suggest that falling moss mats act like magic carpets that carry mites through their arboreal world.

Like a person accumulating experience and memories with age, a tree accumulates other organisms as it grows and develops a more complex shape. With time, the mass of other organisms living on and within old trees can start to approach the mass of the trees themselves. When Antonie van Leeuwenhoek constructed his microscope and examined a drop of pond water, he was astonished to find the water droplet swarming with miniature life. So can we continually astonish ourselves by examining a forest, an individual tree, and a small portion of that tree in closer and closer detail, discovering progressively more minute and interconnected life sharing materials and energy through intricate collaborations honed by evolution.

Much larger, mobile creatures such as marbled murrelets also make a home among the canopy epiphytes, constructing nests in shallow depressions of lichens or moss high above the ground. The murrelet is a small brown-and-white seabird that flies several miles inland from the coast to nest in old-growth conifer forests, seeking out large trees with more potential nest platforms, greater moss cover on branches, and a closed canopy.

Other birds nesting in western redcedar are perhaps more expected than a seabird. Northern spotted owls nest in cavities in living and dead trees and on platforms built by other birds or animals or resulting from the accumulation of plant debris on a branch. Most nests are in the crown of a living tree in a stand with a relatively closed canopy. Redcedars are among the trees chosen by these owls, which perch on tree branches at night, silently scanning the forest for their prey of small rodents.

Pileated woodpeckers, which nest and roost in large cavities of snags and living trees, also frequently choose western redcedar. Although redcedar is less susceptible to fungal pathogens than some other conifers, heartwood fungi do attack living redcedars. During the later stages of wood decay by the fungi, the rot column forms a tubular shape that can extend eighty feet up the trunk and spread into large branches. These large cavities are perfect for the pileated woodpeckers, which can reach twenty inches in body length. The woodpeckers also prefer enough space to create multiple openings in a nesting cavity, which facilitate escape from predators such as hawks, owls, martens, and weasels. In addition to providing large heart-rot cavities, western redcedars may be particularly important because these long-lived trees can provide nest and roost sites for decades to centuries. Each nesting pair of woodpeckers excavates a nest cavity in a different tree each year, leaving a trail of cavities that other birds and animals such as flying squirrels can also use.

Songbirds partition the canopy by species. Pine siskins, small finches with brown and cream stripes, seek seeds and insects in the upper canopy, where other agile hunters seek flying insects on the wing—common nighthawks at dawn and dusk and Vaux's swifts during the day. In the midcanopy, intrepid gray jays rear chicks in the dark of winter; red crossbills pry out seeds tightly held in cones; and flashes of bright yellow reveal hermit warblers seeking insects and spiders. Varied thrushes, looking festive in Halloween colors of orange and black, eat insects and arthropods from the leaf litter during breeding season. These thrushes prefer the lower canopy, in which house wrens also seek insects and nest in cavities. Northern goshawks use the aerial agility conferred by short, broad wings and a long, rudder-like tail to chase birds and small mammal prey through the canopy.

Bats use the old-growth canopy, too, starting at ground level early in the evening and shifting to higher levels as the night goes on. Smaller bats with shorter, broader wings can fly deftly through the canopy, but larger bats prefer to hunt in open parts of the forest and above the canopy.

Red tree voles are unique among small mammals in being canopy dwellers. The voles nest at the top of old-growth Douglas-firs in Oregon, where they eat needles and drink dew. Before eating the needles, the voles carefully remove the fine resin ducts, leaving a pile of what look like coarse, straight hairs, which they then discard or use for nest lining.

Northern flying squirrels—attractive little mammals with large dark eyes, a rounded head, and small ears—eat mushrooms and truffles on the forest floor but nest in tree cavities. They use epiphytes for nesting material, as do several types of birds, and in winter several squirrels may huddle together for warmth in a shared nest. Flying squirrels of course do not fly—they glide through the forest canopy by night. Think of the dexterity needed to maneuver among dense branches and foliage. A squirrel can launch itself with a running start or from a stationary position. Bringing its legs under its body, retracting its head, and then propelling itself out into space, the squirrel forms an X shape with its legs, allowing its patagium to stretch into a square. The patagium is a membrane, the name of which comes from the Latin *patagium* and the ancient Greek *patageion*, referring to the gilded edging of a woman's tunic. Imagine if you had a thin but wide flap of skin from each wrist down the length of your body to your ankle. Mostly, you could keep this wonderful appendage modestly folded and out of the way, until you were ready to glide through the air. The little squirrel is in a sense the Superman of the forest, complete with flying cape. Once in a glide, the squirrel descends at angles of thirty to forty degrees and can make ninety-degree turns around obstacles if needed. Just before reaching a landing spot, the squirrel raises its flattened tail, which abruptly changes its trajectory to upward, and points its limbs forward to create a parachute with the patagium. This reduces the shock of landing. Despite their dexterity, flying squirrels are vulnerable to predation by spotted and other types of owls, as well as martens, lynx, and red fox.

Pacific fishers, a member of the weasel family, also seek out old trees for their dens, venturing out by night to eat hares, rodents, birds, and even porcupines. A fisher is about thirty to forty inches long, with a bushy tail at one end and small, rounded ears, small eyes, and a pointed snout at the other. Although an excellent tree climber, the fisher spends much of its time hunting on the forest floor, retracting its claws as needed. The animal, which is typically solitary, looks as though it is half in shadow: the fisher's fur darkens from a hoary gold or silver hue on the head and shoulders to black on the hind legs and tail. Although they nest in trees, fishers seek out downed logs for resting sites, as well as ground burrows and snow dens for resting during winter.

Then there are the full-time inhabitants of the forest floor in a Pacific Northwest old-growth stand, especially the salamanders. Brown northwestern salamanders nine to ten inches long live in underground burrows, feeding on invertebrates and other amphibians such as tadpoles. Paradoxically named giant salamanders, which are actually smaller than northwestern salamanders, live under bark and logs on the forest floor. Torrent salamanders live in small, clear brooks running through the forest.

To be an amphibian—such as a salamander—is to live uniquely exposed to the dangers of the terrestrial world. Reptiles have scales to protect them; birds have feathers that can shed water and be fluffed for greater insulation; mammals have fur. The entire body of an amphibian is covered in permeable skin that makes the animal reliant on habitats in or near water or other cool, damp places. Some species of salamanders, along with frogs, are fully aquatic throughout their lives. Other salamanders seek water intermittently or are entirely terrestrial once they become adults. A salamander's thin skin is permeable because it serves as a respiratory membrane. The cost of breathing along the entire body is the danger of desiccation when on land.

A salamander's vulnerability is reduced in other ways. The skin is well supplied with glands that create a coating of mucus over the animal's body. This mucus keeps the skin moist and helps the salamander control its body temperature, as well as protecting against bacterial infections and molds. The mucus likely reduces friction when a salamander swims and, by making the body slippery, may make it harder for predators to catch. When threatened, some species of salamander can excrete toxic chemicals from glands in their neck, back, and tail. These chemicals can be deadly to small animals hoping to make a meal of the salamander but are likely only to irritate human skin. The most impressive quality of salamanders, however, is their ability to regenerate lost limbs and damaged body parts, a capability that scientists would dearly love to extend to humans.

The tendency of salamanders to shelter in damp, rotting wood, and then to emerge when the logs are burned in a fireplace, led to the misconception that salamanders were created from flames. Pliny the Elder claimed that a salamander could also extinguish fire, and the myth was perpetuated by Saint Augustine in the fifth century and by many subsequent writers. Once fascinated by salamanders for their apparent association with fire, humans remain fascinated by these creatures for their potential to guide us in developing limb regeneration for injured people.

Columbian black-tailed deer come into the forest surrounding the redcedar to browse on epiphytes growing low on the trees. Black bears come through in search of food, from the small voles and shrews of the forest floor to insects in decaying

A dark brown northwestern salamander gently cradled in the hands of a river scientist.

wood. Martens, which can den on the forest floor or up in the canopy, also prey on voles. Other predators of voles and rodents include ermine weasels and their larger cousins, long-tailed weasels, which do not dig their own burrows. Instead, adding insult to injury, these weasels use the nests of rodents that they kill on the forest floor or in snags and then line the nest chamber with the skins and underfur of the unfortunate rodents. Minks move between the river channel, where they catch fish, and the forest floor, where they prey on rodents, amphibians, and birds.

The majestic tree that grew from a small seed forms a portion of an intricate web of life extending from the microscopic organisms that can capture food from the air and the soil to the megafauna of black bears in the forest and the coho and Chinook salmon swimming up the Queets to spawn. The longer it lives, the more the redcedar contributes. As the surrounding forest matures and ages, more and more organisms take up residence on and within the trees, in the understory, and in the soil. The trees store more carbon, and they and their epiphytes capture more nitrogen. If a forest could speak, it might indeed say, "Grow old along with me! The best is yet to be."

Death

If all goes well, a western redcedar can live for more than a thousand years. Because it lives so long, some damage is inevitable. Windthrow takes some of the neighbors. Although redcedar generally suffers little harm from insects, gall midge affects some redcedar seeds, a weevil and a leaf blight can injure or kill seedlings, and the western cedar borer can harm mature trees. More than two hundred species of fungi can live on western redcedar, and some of them damage the tree. Although redcedar is less susceptible to deadly attacks than many of the surrounding tree species, root, butt, and trunk rots damage mature trees, especially in old-growth stands. None of these dangers account for the death of the western redcedar of this tale. Instead, death comes to the tree from the force of flowing water while the tree is still a relatively young three hundred years old.

The Queets rises in flood during one cold, wet week in December. Rain dropping from the canopy makes a steady patter back in the forest, but the roar of turbulent water drowns all other sounds close to the river. At the outside of each meander bend the racing flow twists and spirals so that the water cuts into the stream bank like a buzz saw. Masses of sediment from the eroding bank drop into the water, the thunk and splash of their falling lost in the noise of the rushing water. The helical current that removes sediment from the outside of each bend also drops sediment to form a point bar on the inside of the bend. As the meander cuts steadily across the valley floor during the flood, the relatively high, old portion of the floodplain on which the redcedar grows is undercut. The entire tree topples into the channel. Thousands of pounds of tree, lichens, bryophytes, and ferns—down it all comes with a crash that would reverberate through the valley if river, wind, and rain were not already making so much noise.

The river is about 150 feet wide and the tall tree falls into it at an angle. The root wad of the tree acts like an anchor, dragging on the stream bed as the tree moves a short distance downstream to the head of the next point bar. There the tree comes to rest with the root wad at the upstream end. The enormous branches, many of them the size of small trees, bristle up from the floodwaters. Their dense foliage and still-attached epiphytes comb the water for smaller pieces of wood carried on the current, and a mass of branches and leaves quickly starts to accumulate on the upstream side of the fallen redcedar.

Every flood large enough to start moving the cobbles on the bed of the Queets creates a maelstrom for the microbes and insects living there. Turbulent water carries sand grains like so many mobile sandblasters, and the cobbles of the bed roll over and grind against one another. Many smaller organisms die. Others are dislodged and carried far downstream in a process stream ecologists refer to as drift loss. The drifting refugees may survive, but they will not work their way back upstream until they emerge from the water as winged adults (and maybe not even then). Any point of stability during the flood creates a refuge for the smallest creatures, so the logjam shelters a greater density of aquatic insects than the nearby sediment. Some of these refugees remain on the jam, and others are the pioneers who recolonize the disturbed stream bed after the floodwaters recede.

Life after Death I: Episodic Loops between the Channel and Floodplain
High river flows deposit another large tree with a root wad beside the redcedar. These key pieces form the nucleus of a logjam as smaller pieces of wood rack up against them. More and more wood pieces pile against the upstream side of the jam, which eventually rises twenty feet above the channel. As the floodwaters recede, sand, silt, and clay settle in and around the jam.

A long, narrow pool is now present upstream from the logjam on the channel side. On the bank side, plants take root in the fine sediment and organic matter trapped by the logjam. First come the willows and alders, then with time the conifers. Sediment and growing plants knit the logjam into the floodplain on one side while the channel bend continues to move gradually away from the jam on the other side. Flows that spill over the channel banks deposit more silt and clay on top of the jam even as the channel moves farther toward the other side of the valley floor. Gradually, the redcedar log is buried within the floodplain.

Even when the log is buried, the decaying wood continues to provide food for invertebrates. Although the creatures living on buried logs are not as diverse or as abundant as those living on wood at the surface, fungi and bacteria grow on the wood. Invertebrates find the buried treasure and graze on the fungi and bacteria. All these organisms are present in the sediment underlying the channel and floodplain wherever circulating subterranean water helps provide dissolved oxygen and nutrients, but the community of the very small is richer where there is buried wood.

The Queets River erodes a small portion of its floodplain every year. On average, any portion of the floodplain has a three hundred- to five-hundred-year period of stability between when it is deposited and when it is next eroded, so the redcedar remains buried for centuries. Burial slows the processes of decomposition that attacked the fallen spruce in Colorado, but the buried log does gradually decay. While the log is beneath the surface, the logjam around it forms a hard point in the floodplain. The subterranean pile of wood resists bank erosion and sideways movement of the channel better than does the surrounding sediment. The buried wood

Logjams. In the upper photo, the root wads of trees recently introduced to the channel through bank erosion lie on end, forming obstructions that effectively catch other material downstream. In the lower photo, trees that have been stripped of their bark and most of their branches during transport down the river have collected into a jam at the head of a forested bar in the river (flow is from right to left).

A decaying snag acting as a nurse log and supporting saplings growing from it.

also provides a source of nutrients and nurse logs to newly germinated seedlings. Patches of mature conifer forest are more likely to develop on the hard points of buried logjams because of the extra nutrients and protection from river erosion. But the river continually moves back and forth across the floodplain, and eventually the mature forest and buried logs will enter the channel when the river returns to this point and erodes the floodplain.

Most of the downed wood in the Queets remains in the river channel for fewer than fifty years, but buried wood exhumed centuries later by bank erosion can be more than a thousand years old. Endless lateral movement by the river creates a mosaic of differently aged surfaces and forest patches on the floodplain that provide habitat for a wide variety of plants and animals. Any point within the vegetation mosaic of the floodplain is likely underlain by at least some old, slowly decaying wood. The woody skeletons of older floodplain forests form a loose, three-dimensional lattice in which river-deposited sediment becomes soil, the rhizosphere develops, and new floodplain forest grows and matures.

After death, the redcedar moves episodically down the Queets toward the ocean, losing a little of itself during each succeeding stage of movement and storage. The river deposited the sediment on which the redcedar germinated, and the river eventually kills the tree by removing the sediment in which it is rooted. First, the redcedar is carried a short distance downstream. Trapped in a logjam, it is then buried in the floodplain for centuries. Eventually the log is re-eroded and transported another few hundred feet downstream before being trapped in another logjam, covered with soil for more than a century, and then eroded and carried downstream yet again.

Over half the large conifers that the Queets introduces to the channel through bank erosion are deposited in more than three locations and move more than a mile downstream during a period of hundreds of years before finally disintegrating. Some of the logs have an even more punctuated journey: 10 percent of the trees that fall into the channel have seven distinct places of burial and subsequent erosion over a distance of more than seven miles. Essentially, the redcedar alternates between brief intervals of floating or being dragged downstream in the channel and long years of resting on or within the floodplain.

The episodic journey of the redcedar downstream is accompanied by decay of the log while buried in the floodplain and abrasion and breakage while moving down the channel. In each portion of the journey, the log that was once a giant redcedar grows shorter and narrower. Nutrients held in the wood are redistributed among myriad other organisms. During the log's phases of resting on the floodplain before being covered in soil, wood-boring insects enter it, including colonies of Pacific dampwood termites.

On warm evenings during late summer and autumn, the quiet air beneath the forest canopy is stirred by the wing rattling of swarms of termites emerging from holes in damp logs and taking flight. This is the nuptial, colonizing flight of the termites. Termites are weak fliers and seldom travel far. Many are eaten by bats. Survivors cast their wings and, on encountering an individual of the opposite sex that has also cast its wings, form a pair. The female leads the male to a fallen tree in which to excavate a small nuptial chamber and copulate. Not any tree will do. Fungi within a rotting tree create chemicals that termites can detect, and the insects follow these chemical clues to find a suitable home for the new colony. The new termite colony will eventually consist of up to five hundred individuals, each of which can live for several years. The first offspring from the mated pair are sterile workers, but after four years, winged, reproductive individuals are born and go on to found new colonies.

The termites feed on the rotting wood in which they live. Termites can digest wood because of the ecosystem within their guts. Protozoans in the termite's gut engulf wood particles and ferment the cellulose in the wood, creating carbon dioxide, hydrogen, and acetic acid. Acetic acid is absorbed through the wall of the termite's hindgut and oxidized as energy. In essence, the protozoans break down wood into a form that termites can use as food. The termites return the favor by providing in their gut an oxygen-free chamber with food for the protozoans. Both the termite and the protozoans require nitrogen. Wood is not especially rich in nitrogen, although termites consume mostly wood in which fungi supply extra vitamins and nitrogen. If there is a nitrogen deficit, nitrogen-fixing bacteria in a termite's gut make up the difference. This allows the termites to both excavate and eat the wood.

A downed log can be riddled with termite galleries without any external indications of the activity within. The resulting network of passages created by termites is also used by plant roots and by other animals. Bacteria, fungi, collembolans, mites, centipedes, and, eventually, salamanders, voles, shrews, and American shrew-moles find homes and food in the termite galleries. A black bear ripping open a decaying log in search of termites exposes a community within the log's woody tissue, a sub-lignum community, analogous to the subterranean communities of soils.

Once the log is buried, processes of decay slow down. Although fungi can slow-ly degrade the lignin compounds within wood in the absence of oxygen, the faster rates of decomposition by microbes require oxygen. If the wood is saturated when it is buried, bacteria can rapidly attack the nonlignin portions of the wood, but col-onization by wood-degrading bacteria and microfungi occurs more slowly. Conse-quently, much of the progressive mass loss within the western redcedar log occurs while the log is at the surface or being transported in the channel.

When the log is in transport down the channel, it repeatedly hits—and hits hard—other floating logs, living trees along the stream banks, and rocks in the chan-nel. Floating logs can leave a distinctive trail of scarred or sheared-off tree trunks and gouged stream banks in their wake. The logs themselves break, too. Even a recently dead tree with firm wood has fragments banged off during its headlong progress downstream, and soft, decayed wood breaks up faster. The resulting wood chips are then abraded and rounded. Fragments the size of a human hand sometimes assume a flattened, oblong shape that people describe as river teeth. Thin ovals the size of a very small pebble can accumulate along the margins of a channel to form a wood beach.

All of these pieces smaller than a tree trunk move more rapidly downstream, floating on the water surface until trapped in an eddy or the backwater of a logjam, or gently lowered onto the nearest surface as floodwaters recede. Where these small pieces settle on the floodplain, microbes, fungi, and burrowing animals quickly in-corporate the wood fragments into the soil—wood mulch from the river. Where the pieces settle in an eddy or a backwater pool, the larval phase of some types of stream insects can ingest the wood fragments, and the fragments become macroin-vertebrate food.

A macroinvertebrate is an animal without a backbone that can be seen without a microscope. Macroinvertebrates form the middle of a stream food web. At the base in shaded streams are inputs of organic matter from the adjacent floodplain in the form of fallen leaves, needles, and cones, and dissolved organic matter carried in surface runoff or groundwater into the channel. In streams receiving abundant sun-light, photosynthetic plants such as algae, mosses and lichens, and rooted vascular plants like cattails and water lilies form the most visible base of the stream food web.

The biofilm community forms the largely invisible base of a stream food web. Biofilms create the slimy surfaces in rivers. They consist of algae attached to the stream bed, bacteria, fungi, single-celled microscopic animals known as protozoans, and the even smaller micrometazoans. The biofilm spreads like a living ground fog, coating all solid, at least temporarily stationary, surfaces in the channel. Consumers within the biofilm are also the first to use the energy contained in living or dead plant material.

A macroinvertebrate (caddisfly larva) in the pebble-lined, tubular case it has constructed. Here, the insect's legs partly protrude from the open end of the case at left. The insect is perched on a large boulder on the stream bed.

Macroinvertebrates, which form the next level of the food web, include the aquatic larval stage of such familiar insects as mayflies. One might be pardoned for having trouble relating the larva, which slightly resembles a miniature scorpion, to the slender adult mayfly with its long, lacy wings. Other macroinvertebrates look like small worms with whiskers (larval flies) or miniature shrimp (crustaceans without a carapace known as amphipods). Mollusks, leeches, tiny roundworms known as nematodes, and crustaceans from the nearly invisible to large crayfish round out the list of macroinvertebrates in streams. Some of them live mostly at the water surface, while others take the full water column for their home. Many cling to sediment or logs on the stream bed, and some go all the way down into the hyporheic zone beneath the channel and the floodplain. When curious stream ecologists first pumped hyporheic water up through a shallow well on a floodplain in Montana, imagine their surprise at seeing larval insects nearly the length of a human finger coming out with the water. Although mostly tiny, macroinvertebrates can account for more than half the total biomass within a stream—take that, salmon!

The aquatic insects in the macroinvertebrate community can be classified by how they obtain food. Shredders such as the larvae of some species of caddisflies feed on nonwoody bits of organic matter like leaves or sunken fruits and flowers. Collectors, including the larvae of some species of stoneflies, feed on smaller bits of organic matter. They gather these bits from surface deposits on the stream bed or filter them from the water column using either fine hairs on their bodies or silk nets that they spin and hold up in the current, very like a human fishing by holding a seine net in the current. Grazers, including the larvae of some species of mayflies and caddisflies, scrape single-celled algae from the biofilm. Predators like dragonfly larvae and water beetles eat other organisms. Many larval insect members of the macroinvertebrate community become food for fish or ouzels. The insects that survive to emerge as winged adults either complete their life cycle or feed riparian birds, spiders, and bats.

Why do woody bits get excluded from the list of shredder food? Because not all forms of carbon are equally available to organisms. Labile (from Latin *labi*, "to fall") carbon occurs in compounds that are easily broken down. This is carbon in sugars, proteins, and compounds that are readily used by bacteria and microbes. Refractory (from Latin *refractarius*, "stubborn") carbon occurs in structurally complex compounds such as lignin from woody plants, pollen, or humic acids from soils. Refractory carbon, as the name implies, is difficult for organisms to break down and metabolize. So the tiny wood fragments are the stubborn bits that remain after biofilm and macroinvertebrate feeding. In headwater streams, this material can compose nearly 90 percent of the dead organic matter stored in backwater pools, but this is still a small fraction of total organic carbon storage when compared to the carbon stored in the logs of logjams or in the adjacent floodplain soil.

The wood fragments are not necessarily stored very long, even if they are saturated and rest on the stream bed. Any shift in the bed configuration, such as movement of large wood or an increase in velocity as discharge in the stream rises, can send the wood fragments on their way once more. Eventually, some of the fragments flow from the mouth of the Queets and into the Pacific Ocean.

The redcedar of this tale grew about thirty river miles upstream from the coast and does not make it to the ocean as a discernible log. Along this distance, the Queets follows a sinuous course that alternates between stretches where mature conifer forest shoulders up to the channel, and wider portions of valley floor where the Queets braids among sand and gravel bars and patches of younger, deciduous forest. In the wide areas, the bends of the former channel are clearly visible from above as differences in the type and height of trees. The Queets follows its irregularly winding course downstream past a series of tributary junctions—Coal Creek, Sams River, Boulder Creek, Matheny Creek, and Tacoma Creek—and then past the Clearwater River and the boundary of Olympic National Park. The final seven miles of the river, past the town of Queets, include a long, generous meander.

The lower Queets River, near the Pacific coast, with a logjam at the entrance of a secondary channel at right. Flow is toward the rear of the image.

About a mile before it enters the Pacific, the Queets divides into distributary channels. At the very end, one of the distributaries takes a sharp bend and flows parallel to the coast, as though reluctant to merge with the ocean. The beach between this distributary and the surf zone is thick with driftwood aligned by the currents of river, waves, and tides. Some of the wood fragments are trapped here. Other fragments are swept slightly down shore into the equally wood-rich and partly vegetated back beach just north of the river mouth. Together with the larger pieces of wood delivered by the Queets to the beach, the wood fragments play a crucial role in the ecosystems of sandy beaches.

Life after Death II: The Beach

The coast near the mouth of the Queets is commonly an environment of hues of gray: pewter-gray sea; sky the gray of rain clouds; a cobble shingle of pale gray-wacke stones; pale gray weathered driftwood; shorebirds with gray-and-white plumage. Only the white surf and the green vegetation inland interrupt the world of gray as a light breeze brings in a fine, misting rain. Big, barkless skeletons of trees lie piled against the seaward edge of vegetated dunes. Some of the driftwood trunks still bristle with branches; others are worn and smoothed to a nubbin of root wad at the end of a fat cylinder of trunk. A less worn root wad is more like an open umbrella attached to the trunk and can extend more than twenty feet across. The most abraded and polished pieces reveal the swirls and spirals of the wood grain.

The accumulations of driftwood record the power and the quiet spots of the sea. Pieces of dead wood may be violently flung up onto the beach by incoming waves, but in repose they suggest a pause and a regrouping, and here the wood forms shelter and refuge for seedlings and animals.

Driftwood logs or even smaller pieces of wood are harder for wind and water to move than are grains of sand. Consequently, driftwood forms points of at least temporary stability on a sandy beach subject to continual breezes, not to mention swash and backwash, high and low tides, and storm surges. Logs trap sand, bits of dead terrestrial and marine plants, and plant propagules being transported along the beach face. Wood can accumulate so much sand that, on narrow beaches, dunes form temporarily where driftwood accumulates at the base of storm-cut cliffs. On wider beaches, driftwood can trap moving sand across a zone more than six hundred feet wide and create embryo dunes. Beach grasses and sedges able to survive on shifting sands can then help stabilize the dunes.

Some beach plant communities can survive only where driftwood is present. The sand trapped by the driftwood forms a better germination site for plants, many of which tend to have higher survival and reproduction rates where driftwood is present. The sheltering presence of wood also traps more seeds and a wider variety of seeds, creating greater potential for plants to germinate near the logs.

Fungi can colonize the more humid underside of the driftwood, attracting springtails, arachnids, potworms, and beetles that feed on the fungi. Crustose lichens can grow on any part of the wood, and some of these lichen species live only on driftwood. Larvae of sand scarab beetles living on the beach sand develop better in the presence of driftwood. And then there are the sandhoppers, sometimes misleadingly called sand fleas. Sandy beaches are full of these little crustaceans that eat mostly dead and decaying algae and other plants and animals. Some species live in the wrack—algae, kelp, bits of jellyfish, or whatever else washes up with the tide. Other species burrow in the sand. A few live in driftwood.

Some species of sandhoppers essentially never leave the shelter of driftwood, which allows them to coexist close to other species that prefer open sand. Some of the sandhopper species that prefer driftwood eat whatever detritus is reachable from the safety of the wood, whereas others eat the decomposing wood itself.

The fancy name for the seven species of sandhoppers known to eat wood, and for any other organism that eats wood, is "xylophage" (from the Greek *xulon*, "wood," and *phagos*, "one who eats"). These species are smaller than other sandhoppers, which may reflect the poor quality of their food compared to other wrack that the waves leave behind. Smaller size also allows these malnourished sandhoppers

Driftwood logs accumulating at the base of a coastal cliff near the mouth of the Queets River. Branches and bark are gone from this wood, which is abraded and weathered to a pale gray color.

to occupy the burrows made by gribbles, which are tiny marine crustaceans that bore into wood. Evidence of poor diet comes from the fact that sandhoppers eating driftwood move much more slowly than those eating other types of food, as well as being smaller. Why evolve to be small and ill nourished? Wood wrack is not all ruin. The driftwood protects the sandhoppers from being eaten by shorebirds, and the sandhoppers can disperse widely when they hitchhike on floating wood. Also, the driftwood food lasts for many years, even if it is not especially nutritious. The sandhoppers actually obtain their food via bacteria decomposing the wood or other wrack on the beach, and these bacterial communities differ between wood, algae, and other forms of wrack.

In addition to helping to stabilize and shape the beach, driftwood can inoculate the beach with life. Logs floating down a river contain hitchhikers from microbes and algae to mollusks such as small snails. Some of these organisms may survive the change from freshwater to a salty beach.

The dissolved remnants of wood from the Queets also contribute food to coastal organisms. River water flushed into the surf zone enters a distinctive ecosystem.

There are no attached plants in the high-energy environment and shifting sands of the surf zone. Instead, single-celled algae known as diatoms live in the water. Although microscopic, diatoms do not just float passively wherever the waves take them but instead follow a regular twenty-four-hour cycle. Diatoms accumulate at the water surface during the day as a result of rip currents that concentrate the tiny algae in certain areas. During the afternoon, the diatoms form a sticky mucus sheath that catches floating particles of clay. The extra weight of the mucus and clay causes the diatom cells to sink, allowing rip currents to carry them behind the breaker line. The diatoms accumulate near the bottom of the water column or in the sediment before shedding the mucus sheath and rising to the surface once more in the morning. On rising, the diatoms are transported into the inner surf zone by wave action. By comparison, human surfers paddling their boards out and then riding the waves back at the surface seem a little flat. The diatoms make a three-dimensional journey every twenty-four hours, moving seaward along the bottom in their self-made coats, then shedding the coats, rising to the surface, and riding the waves back toward shore.

This diatom cycle fuels three other food webs in the surf zone. The first involves the community of bacteria, protozoans, and equally small creatures known as interstitial fauna because they live within tiny spaces between sand grains beneath the waves. Life in the interstices—it sounds like an avant-garde movie. Waves flush organic material into the sand, and mucus sloughed off by diatoms contributes food, allowing the interstitial fauna to consume nearly a fifth of what the diatoms produce. Because sand in the surf zone is continually being turned over, interstitial fauna can penetrate deep into the sand.

The second food web based on the diatoms involves creatures large enough to be seen with the naked eye (barely, in some cases). This group consumes about 10 percent of the diatoms. The creatures of this food chain range from small zooplankton, which are floating organisms that eat single-celled algae, to bottom-dwelling organisms such as clams and mussels, and fish.

The final food web is the so-called microbial loop in the water column, which—despite its small size—gets the lion's share and consumes more than half the diatoms. In this food web, bacteria and microzooplankton eat diatoms. Flagellates (swimming protozoans) then eat the bacteria and microzooplankton.

If diatoms are like miniature surfers in their movements across the surf zone, then the members of the three food webs are the great white sharks.

The carbon that fuels these food webs comes from photosynthesis by the diatoms, but the nitrogen necessary for all the organisms enters in dissolved form via groundwater or river water. Some of this nitrogen in the river water was once a part of the western redcedar. The river water also carries dissolved carbon from the big tree, and the carbon and nitrogen benefit many coastal organisms. Clams from portions of a coast influenced by plumes of freshwater where a river flows into the ocean, for example, contain different isotopes of carbon and nitrogen than clams away from a river's influence. These differences indicate that the clams in the river plume are consuming dissolved nutrients derived from the soils and forests of the river's catchment.

The small wood bits carried to the beach play their part, too, despite their recalcitrant carbon. They can increase the beach sand's ability to retain moisture and provide an organic substrate for seedlings to germinate in. Where so-called beach cleaning removes driftwood and other organic matter that some people find unattractive, the extent of plant cover and native plant abundance and species diversity decline dramatically, as do the number and diversity of invertebrates including small crustaceans and worms.

Bottom-dwelling invertebrates including bristle worms, crustaceans, mollusks, starfish, and sea urchins, along with flatfish such as sole, also feed on bits of organic matter coming from the river. Other sources of labile carbon, such as red alder leaves that accumulate in tide pools, remain more palatable than wood fragments. Nevertheless, some marine organisms may ingest the tiniest fragments of wood containing fungi and bacteria to get at the microorganisms. Other fish then come to prey on the invertebrates eating the terrestrial organic matter.

Thus, in so many ways, does the western redcedar contribute to the channel and floodplain of the river and to the beach and nearshore ecosystems after its death. As with the Engelmann spruce, the processes of decay and release of the constituent parts of the redcedar last longer than the tree's lifetime. Countless other organisms benefit from the tree's enduring legacy.

This legacy depends on the continuation of natural cycles. A forest in which trees can continue to grow for hundreds of years provides the enormous individual trees that can block even a large river sufficiently to create a huge, stable logjam. A river in which bends meander back and forth across the forested floodplain can erode its banks and recruit trees to the channel, transport the fallen trees downstream, and deposit sediment around stable logs and logjams. A floodplain with newly deposited patches of sediment supplies germination sites for trees and shrubs of different species that eventually form a mosaic of vegetation communities. That mosaic provides habitat for a wide variety of insects, birds, amphibians, and mammals, not to mention canopy epiphytes and the subterranean community of the rhizosphere.

And a river that flows unimpeded to the ocean carries nutrients, organisms, and wood to the beach and the surf zone. When people disrupt any of these interconnected exchanges by cutting forests, channelizing and damming rivers, removing downed wood, and clearing beaches of driftwood, they impoverish the ecosystems that rely on the long lives, and equally long afterlives, of trees.

The Third Tree: Traveler

A Balsam Poplar along the Kechika River of Canada

Balsam poplar (*Populus balsamifera*) is a tree of the northlands, a species that grows farther north than any other deciduous tree in North America. From the Atlantic shores of Newfoundland and Labrador to the Yukon Territory and into Alaska, balsam poplars grow on upland sites and, especially, along the floodplains of rivers. The tree's distribution forms a solid band from central Alaska east-southeast across Canada to the Great Lakes. Narrow fingers of poplar territory extend southward from the main band along river valleys such as tributaries of the Mackenzie River, which flows north to the Arctic Ocean.

Populus derives from the Latin word for "people" or "nation." The word became associated with cottonwoods and poplars because these trees were commonly planted around public meeting places of the Roman empire, although the balsam poplar is native to North America.

Eighteen thousand years ago, the great Laurentide Ice Sheet reached its maximum extent across Canada and the northern fringe of the continental United States. Following the northward retreat of the ice, balsam poplars also moved northward. Individual trees, of course, moved not at all. But their wind-borne seeds progressively colonized newly exposed land as the ice melted and flowed down a thousand meltwater channels, each of which was flanked by fresh, moist sediment ideal for poplar germination. The genetics of contemporary balsam poplars suggest that the ancestral population existed south of the ice sheet in the central United States. Three genetically related subpopulations exist today in the northern, central, and eastern parts of the poplar's range. The central subpopulation is likely most genetically similar to the ancestral population. The northern subpopulation may have colonized deglaciated regions more quickly, perhaps along the ice-free corridor that opened between the Laurentide Ice Sheet to the east and the Cordilleran Ice Sheet covering the western mountains. This corridor opened about twelve thousand years ago, permitting plants to migrate into the northwestern part of North America while the northeastern part remained under ice. Interior Alaska was also too dry to host an ice sheet during the Pleistocene, and balsam poplars may have remained there throughout the ice ages. Today, balsam poplars across North America have relatively low genetic diversity, strongly suggesting recent migration outward from a small, central population.

One of the fingers of balsam poplars extending southward includes the Kechika River in Canada, a tributary of the Liard River and thus of the great Mackenzie, which the Liard joins downstream from Great Slave Lake. On the left bank of the Kechika, at 59°33′ N, stands a tall bluff. The channel, which is about 650 feet wide, meanders broadly across a valley floor that is more than a mile wide—the river has room to move. Much of the valley floor steps up from abandoned, filled, overgrown channels to low terraces. Each of these abandoned channels and terraces records some portion of the history of the Kechika's movement. At this spot, however, the channel butts hard against the adjacent uplands, gnawing away at the base of a steep slope along the outside of a meander bend. The collision deforms all parties: the apex of the river bend is flattened and the whole bend has a squashed, asymmetrical form. The hillslope is progressively undercut and episodically collapses into the river in a small landslide, delivering some of the sediment that gives the Kechika its turbid, greenish-gray color.

The forested top of the bluff has a rumpled appearance that contrasts with the more smoothly rounded low mounds of the uplands farther from the river. Up a tributary valley, the rumpled surface takes the distinctly serpentine form of an esker created by sediment deposited along a sinuous river flowing beneath the Laurentide Ice Sheet. Under pressure caused by the weight of overlying material, ice at the base of a glacier melts at temperatures below freezing. Whether a small alpine glacier or the largest ice sheet, glacial ice is not a solid block but something more like a mostly frozen slush. Meltwater throughout the mass of ice helps lubricate the glacier and keep it moving downslope. So much meltwater can collect under the ice that large streams form between the ice and the underlying bedrock. While the glacier is present, these ice-buried streams carry and deposit sediment. When the glacier disappears, the sinuous lines of sediment deposited along the stream channel form ridges. The surrounding smoothly rounded uplands, now forested, are the subdued bedrock topography left after sediment carried within the ice planed down the underlying rock.

Below the bluff, bands of trees parallel to the left bank of the channel record

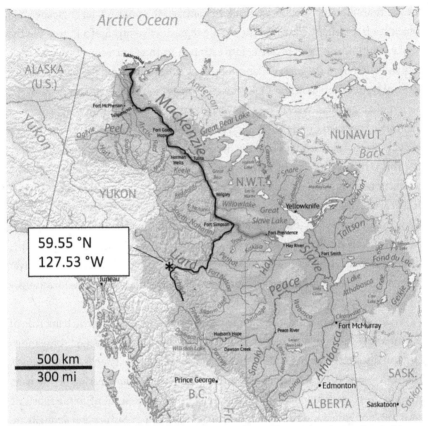

Map of the location of the balsam poplar along the Kechika River within the Mackenzie River drainage. The heavy line indicates the long path of the poplar log after death, down the Liard and then the Mackenzie to the Arctic Ocean.

the battle between the channel and the resistant slope above it. The Kechika has moved over time toward the right across the valley bottom, shifting the point at which the channel impinges on the bluff. As the channel moves, vegetation colonizes the newly deposited river sediment left behind. As on the Queets, the Kechika erodes portions of the stream banks and topples their mature trees into the channel, but in compensation it deposits fresh sediment elsewhere and creates ideal tree-germination sites. Here the balsam poplar of this tale begins its life.

Germination and Seedling

The parents of the tree in this tale grow just upstream along the Kechika. They begin to flower in May, before their leaves regrow. The Engelmann spruce and western redcedar, like all conifers, are gymnosperms—seed-bearing vascular plants in which the seeds are not enclosed in an ovary. In contrast, the poplar is an angiosperm in which seeds are enclosed within the female reproductive organ of a flower. On the poplar, multiple tiny flowers cluster into each two-to-three-inch-long male or female catkin. Pollen from the male catkins must blow onto seeds from the female catkins for seed fertilization to occur. Once the seeds mature, the tree releases them over a period of at least two weeks. Each tiny seed is attached to a tuft of long, silky hair that carries the seed on the wind like a hot-air balloon. On windy days, the crowds of flying seeds can resemble snow flurries.

This is the start of a great lottery for each seed. It might be carried upward by a convection current and blown far away, or deposited on a surface high above the river that is too dry for the seed to germinate. It might travel only a short distance and fall within a stand of mature poplar trees, there to germinate and then die quickly for lack of sunlight. It might land in the water and float far, far downstream, for the seed can remain viable for more than a month and a little seed is nothing for a river to carry. The seed of this tale travels about a mile downstream and lands fortuitously on a newly deposited bar at the edge of the Kechika.

The seed lands in a crust of sand and exposed algae left along the bank side of the bar as the last high flow receded. Both the sand and the algae retain some moisture and the seed germinates immediately and aboveground. Time is of the essence. The seed's embryonic leaves expand within twenty-four hours. A ring of fine hairs grows at the root-stem junction, and these hairs anchor the seedling to the substrate until the root grows and establishes a stronger roothold. Moisture and sunlight are key now: the presence of both allows the seedling to grow rapidly. A leaf grows just above the embryonic leaves, then another leaf grows.

The leaves of a deciduous tree differ from the needles of a conifer. The leaf blade consists of a central tissue, the mesophyll, surrounded by upper and lower epidermis. The mesophyll contains the chlorophyll molecules that convert light energy into carbohydrates. One main vein and various orders of smaller veins are present. The finest veinlets infiltrate the mesophyll to collect the products of photosynthesis. Only the lower epidermis contains the stomata where carbon dioxide is taken up and water vapor and oxygen are released. The epidermis is covered with wax and cuticle to restrict water loss from the stomata and protect them from drying. Despite the different structures, the poplar's leaves share with the spruce's needles a marvelous set of adaptations to both protect and facilitate the primary function of photosynthesis.

By the end of the first summer, as many as a dozen leaves may have grown, the roots may extend five inches, and the seedling may be just over two inches tall. It

A balsam poplar and a close-up of the leaves, both from Creative Commons.

may not sound like much, but all this differentiation into distinctive tissues of leaf, stem, and root and the initial production of energy via photosynthesis reflect a busy season for the little plant. At this diminutive size, the poplar faces its first northern winter.

Under challenging conditions, it helps to have an older relative to lean on, or even an older version of oneself. Consequently, like other plants in the *Populus* genus, balsam poplar also relies on vegetative reproduction. New stems can originate from intact or broken roots, from stumps, and from buried stems and branches. Growth of suckers from the roots can colonize areas around a mature poplar and create a clone with dozens of genetically identical plants that covers thousands of square feet. Scientists in Canada find that when individual plants in this clonal network experience stresses such as insect infestation or drought, other plants within the network can share resources via these root connections and help the stressed plant survive. Although this strategy of reproducing by suckers can allow established stands to extend into newly created floodplains, expansion of a clone is most useful in dry sites that limit seedling establishment, or at the northern or elevational limits of the poplar. Vegetative reproduction means that the new stems can rely on the older plant to which they remain connected, but the genetically identical plants may also be more susceptible to disease or insects that take down the entire network of clones. So, despite the rigors of winter, the new seedling and its seedling neighbors that result from sexual reproduction represent the best chance of establishing poplars on the river bar.

During the seedling's second growing season, more sediment is deposited on the bar. Fortunately, the stem of the small plant is not buried more than a fraction of an inch, but this burial triggers a reaction that will recur throughout the poplar's life. Early root development is downward, but subsequent root growth occurs at higher levels on the repeatedly buried stem in order to keep producing a set of lateral roots close to the ground surface. Basically, as the ground rises with new sediment deposition from the river, the poplar's uppermost layer of lateral roots rises to keep pace. Eventually, the poplar will have multilayered roots growing laterally out from the stem. In this second season, root development on the buried stem occurs within a few weeks.

While still a seedling, the poplar is vulnerable to browsing by moose, deer, and elk. These animals browse the stems but do not eat the leaves. Stems up to two inches in diameter can be broken by moose eating the tops. If the browsing occurs for only a year or two, the tree can recover its form. If severe browsing persists for years, the tree takes the form of a densely branching, stunted shrub. Beavers can also cut poplars along waterways, but their cutting at the base of the stem can allow the seedling to regrow from the roots. The big ungulates and the busy rodents do not feed on the poplar of this tale, and the seedling continues to grow tall and slender.

Sapling

After passing the five-year mark, the poplar expands its roots rapidly, sending them more than twenty feet across the bar. The saturated soil limits how deep the roots grow downward, but the sapling makes up for shallowness with the lateral extent of its root network. These lateral roots both gather nutrients for the growing plant and create a net just below the ground surface that helps stabilize the bar and limit river erosion. Over the next thirty years, the river repeatedly deposits sediment on the bar as the channel gradually migrates away and the bar attaches to the floodplain. This results in six episodes of additional root development on newly buried portions of the tree's lower stem. In total, the lower five feet of the stem are buried, but the tree continues to grow rapidly upward at the crown and to quickly grow new sets of roots.

The soil in which the tree grows now consists of alternating layers of river sediment and organic matter from plant litter dropped by the sapling and its neighbors during quiet times before the next big river flow adds sand and silt. Leaves and other dead bits of plants dropped to the forest floor contain nitrogen, carbon, and other nutrients that are gradually added to the soil as invertebrates and microbes eat and decompose the plant litter. The most important additions of soil nitrogen, however, come from the neighbors. The poplar saplings on the bar mingle with mountain alders and various species of willow. The alders, in particular, are very useful neighbors.

Ecologists describe alders as able to eat rock. The big, showy trees get the credit for the work done by their diminutive friends. Nitrogen-fixing bacteria within nodules in alder roots have enzymes that convert atmospheric nitrogen into ammonia, which then powers alder growth. Root nodules may sound like arthritic joints or warty skin, but the nodules can be a thing of beauty when exposed above the soil. Each nodule shines in a hue of gold to russet, and together they resemble a handful of jewels on the root.

The rock-eating description comes from the ability of the alder-bacteria team to extract calcium and phosphorus from bedrock, in the process accelerating the breakdown of the rock and releasing more nutrients to fuel tree growth. When crushed and dissolved, alder leaves reveal chemical fingerprints from the underlying bedrock in the form of trace elements. Alders contain more of these rock fingerprints than the leaves of adjacent trees. Sucking up nutrients from air and rock, mountain alders and their bacterial coworkers can fix eighteen to fifty-five pounds of nitrogen per acre of ground each year. This is such a high rate of nitrogen fixation relative to what the alders actually need for growth that excess nitrogen accumulates in the soil as nitric acid. Nitric acid is strong enough to dissolve minerals in bedrock, allowing the alders to acquire the rock's calcium and phosphorus. In essence, bacteria in the root nodules of alders extract nitrogen from the air so efficiently that the leftover nitrogen makes the soil acidic enough to dissolve rock, thereby liberating more essential elements for plant growth. The alders share their bounty when their fallen leaves and twigs decompose and release stored nitrogen to the rhizosphere community and the plants that depend on it, including the poplar.

The sapling poplar continues to grow quickly, with a clearly defined main trunk and a conical crown. The tree begins to flower at eight years of age, and each year it produces a large crop of seeds that are released on the wind to meet their fate. By age twenty, the poplar is thirty-five feet tall.

A few animals eat portions of the saplings, although the chemical composition of the resin reduces an animal's ability to digest the cellulose, making balsam poplars less palatable to animals than many other trees. Some woody plants can exude resins, which are chemical compounds that are not soluble in water and harden when exposed to air. Resins can protect a plant from insects and disease or, by tasting bad, from browsing animals. (Resins can also become gems in the form of amber.) Snowshoe hares may eat poplar twigs and stems, but not the buds, which contain the unappealing resin. Girdling by hares or rodents feeding on the cambium can kill saplings and small trees above the girdle, but dormant buds from below the girdle usually form a new stem. Ruffed grouse sometimes eat buds in the winter.

The chemicals that can render poplar unpalatable to some animals also make the plant useful to humans. Poplar is in the Salicaceae plant family, which also includes willows, the source of salicylic acid (used in aspirin). Ancient Greek healers such as Hippocrates and Galen recognized that willow bark could ease pain and fever, and indigenous peoples in North America recognized that balsam poplar sap could be drunk to treat diabetes and high blood pressure. Balsam poplar extract can be rubbed onto skin to treat boils, wounds, and eczema or to relieve the teething pain of babies; sap and bark boiled together can be used to treat asthma; and tincture from the inner bark can reduce fevers and relieve pain from arthritis. During times of desperation, the cambium of poplar also served as "starvation food." Pharmaceutical companies now use balsam poplar extracts in anti-inflammatory and antiaging balms and lotions, and the ability of these extracts to reduce the formation of adipose tissue (body fat) is of great interest in the contemporary human world.

For the chemically protected balsam poplar, the primary dangers for saplings and mature trees nonetheless come from insects. The poplar and willow borer, a rather unattractive cream-and-brown insect that vaguely resembles a flea with a big head; the bronze poplar borer, which creates zigzagging galleries in the cambium as though the insect were following a switchback trail up the tree; and the poplar borer can girdle or badly weaken trees larger than an inch in diameter by tunneling into the main stem and limbs. The forest tent caterpillar, satin moth, gray willow leaf beetle, and aspen leaf beetle all feed on balsam poplar foliage, but the highly resinous buds and leaves of balsam poplar may render them relatively less palatable than those of other trees, which have more of these insects.

The willows and alder trees are temporary neighbors for the poplar. About twenty years after seedlings colonize the bar, poplars assume dominance and retain this status for seventy-five years, forming a nearly pure stand of mature trees. Poplars take over the bar because their faster growth and greater height allow them to shade out the early neighbors. This doesn't seem like a very gracious reward for the efficient nitrogen fixation of the alders, but the dying alders send seeds to colonize newly deposited river sediment. After several decades, the poplars form a dense stand of relatively slender trees on the former bar along the Kechika.

Maturity

Eighty years after landing on the river bar that is now the floodplain, the balsam poplar is a mature tree reaching upward a hundred feet above the ground, with a trunk sixty inches in diameter. The reddish-gray bark that was smooth during the tree's youth has now become thick and furrowed. The smooth leaves are dark green above and silvery on the underside, continually twisting and fluttering in the lightest breeze. The sticky, resinous buds that form each year give off the strong, sweet fragrance that resulted in the balsam poplar being named for the resemblance of its scent to that of balsam fir.

Each year's growth of leaves requires a surge of energy from the tree, an annual drain that a conifer never undergoes. To leaf or to needle? That is the question that trees faced during their long evolutionary history. Why drop all your leaves every autumn and then face the winter months unable to produce your own food through photosynthesis? The waxy cuticle of a conifer needle conserves nutrients and water better than a broad leaf. The green needles can photosynthesize year-round, too, although they produce less energy than a leaf because of their small surface area. Broad leaves create a lot of energy quickly through photosynthesis, but they also lose more water through their stomata than a conifer needle. And the leaves take some of their nutrients with them when they fall from the tree. Given the millions of conifers and the millions of broad-leaved deciduous trees, each strategy clearly works well in some conditions.

The structural framework on which the poplar's leaves grow also differs from that of a conifer. Unlike the central trunk of a conifer, which extends nearly to the top of the tree, the poplar's central trunk extends to a limited height and then divides continually to form a crown of branches of similar dimension, giving rise to a more rounded crown now that the tree is mature. The branches consist of long shoots that allow the crown to grow upward and outward, with short shoots that produce most of the leaves. Growth stops each autumn but resumes in spring as soon as temperatures are high enough.

Decay-causing fungi are present within the poplar stand, as are some minor infections that cause a roughening of the normally smooth bark, or leaf rust, and leaf and twig blight. On the whole, however, the trees are healthy and grow steadily. The stand is starting to display old-growth characteristics, with snags forming pale columns among the living trees and coarse woody debris present on the forest floor, as well as gaps in the canopy. Cavities appear in snags and around diseased areas in living trees.

The stand of poplar is even-aged. Across the floodplain, tree ages vary by fifty years, reflecting the progressive migration of the river, but within this portion of the floodplain the tree ages are all within a couple of years of each other. Many of the group have died, so that the forest is more open. Although feather mosses and lichens may grow on the poplars, the elaborate canopy epiphyte community of the old-growth western redcedar, or even the Engelmann spruce, is not present among these youngsters.

The greater openness of the understory allows shrubs to establish on the floodplain. On the Kechika floodplain, these include the tall red osier dogwood, with its striking red branches and white berries, and its diminutive cousin in the dogwood genus, bunchberry, which has white flowers and scarlet berries. Tall bearberry honeysuckle grows long, tubular orange flowers tipped in yellow that give rise to black berries. American cranberry bush and highbush cranberry bear scarlet fruits rich in vitamin C in the autumn. The delicate pink flowers of prickly rose grow atop thickly thorned stalks. Northern red currant bears translucent red berries in summer and pumpkin-orange leaves come autumn.

Herbaceous plants on the forest floor include the rigid, gritty-stalked horsetails, the delicately feathered seed heads of bluejoint reedgrass, and the clustered white flowers of northern bedstraw. Fireweed raises stalks of magenta flowers, and northern bluebells dangle clusters of elongated blue flowers. The delicate white flowers of red baneberry produce berries that shout *scarlet* among the green foliage. Bog wintergreen, true to its name, maintains green leaves throughout the winter beneath the snow and then in summer raises stalks with delicately pink-and-white-striped flowers. Claspleaf twistedstalk, despite its clumsy common name, is a graceful plant with slender green leaves arranged along stalks from which hang delicate white flowers shaped like whimsical bells with curling rims. Also present in the understory are white spruce saplings. These spruces are the future dominant trees if the river does not reclaim this portion of the floodplain before the spruces have time to mature.

During spring, summer, and autumn, migratory birds move into and past the poplar stand. Although found mostly on larger river bars and wetlands, solitary sandpipers and greater yellowlegs sometimes stop at the unvegetated edge of the poplar's bar to hunt insects and crustaceans. Sandhill cranes pass overhead en route to the north, uttering their distinctive bugling calls as they fly past in small groups. The steady, powerful wings of tundra swans making the long trip to their breeding grounds on the Arctic coast glow white against the blue sky.

Ducks arrive to establish a nest and raise a brood of ducklings. The breeding plumage of the males, in particular, seems suitable for a formal gala. Slashes of white,

Claspleaf twistedstalk in flower.

blue, gray, and chestnut brown decorate the male harlequin ducks, while females retain a more subdued brown with only small patches of white about their heads. Nesting along the cliffsides or in cavities within the floodplain trees, the harlequins forage on the cobble beaches along the Kechika for aquatic insects and small fish. Common mergansers also nest in larger tree cavities along the river. Males and females are equally striking in appearance: the males with a glowing white body, dark green head and neck, and scarlet bill, and the females arrayed in hues of gray and white with a cinnamon-brown head and neck, a short crest, and an orange bill. The brightly colored bills of the mergansers are slender and serrated, well suited to probing stream-bed sediments for fish and aquatic invertebrates. Common goldeneye ducks are smaller bodied and nest in cavities among the poplar trees. Males have an elegantly marked black-and-white body topped by an emerald-green head with a rounded crest that resembles a pompadour hairstyle. Females also sport a pompadour, but the head is brown and the body plumage a mottled gray and white. Their common name comes from their bright yellow eyes. Like the harlequins and mergansers, the goldeneyes feed on aquatic invertebrates and fish. Lesser scaup and other ducks also breed along the river.

Once the little ones hatch, the shallows along the riverbanks grow busy with parents leading flotillas of ducklings or goslings. The appearance of a raptor causes a flurry of frantic paddling and calling, with even the smallest youngsters diving underwater for extended periods, and anguished cries as families regroup after the danger has passed.

The river corridor grows noisier when the belted kingfishers arrive. These slate-gray birds with a white neck band can raise the long feathers on top of their large heads into an imposing crest. At a foot in length, the kingfisher is large enough to be readily noticed, but it is nearly impossible not to notice the bird's piercing, rapidly repeated, rattling calls. For kingfishers, the Kechika provides access to water for feeding and vertical earthen banks for nesting. Numerous perches overhanging the water where a precariously leaning tree is on its way in (very) slow motion into the channel provide ideal habitat for kingfishers, especially as the river water clears after seasonal high flows recede.

Vying with the kingfishers in pugnacity are the Canada geese. The female chooses a spot on the ground with unobstructed views and near water. Here, she constructs a nest in the form of a large open cup made from dry grass, lichens, and mosses and lined with her own downy feathers. The adults and nestlings will eat mostly grasses and sedges growing along the channel, and the adults defend their vulnerable young with startling ferocity. Most of the goose nests are close to the water, but occasionally one can be seen perched in a shallow alcove high on a cliff along the river.

Red-tailed hawks also seek out the river-side forest for breeding, feeding their nestlings mostly on rodents, rabbits, and hares, as well as the occasional bird. And then there are the truly large raptors: bald eagles. The eagles build huge stick nests in a tree adjacent to the river, choosing their own perches in tall trees with wide views. Fish are the primary food of interest, but the eagles will eat birds, invertebrates, and small mammals, either live or as carrion. The shining white plumage on the head of a mature bald eagle makes the bird readily visible from a distance, and during summer and autumn fish migration, the river-side forest is abundantly punctuated with these white exclamation points.

One swallow does not a summer make, but many swallows make a summer along the Kechika. Tree swallows, violet-green swallows, and bank swallows all migrate in for the breeding season, feasting on the abundant flying insects. Tree and violet-green swallows select nest cavities away from the river in coniferous forest. Bank swallows seek vertical banks along the channel to create colonies of multiple nests.

A bank swallow's brown plumage and white underparts can blend well into the sandy cliffs in which the bird nests, but the swallow is commonly too active, too vo-

cal, and too communal for camouflage. Instead, colonies of swallows enliven the riverbanks, whether darting erratically through the air in pursuit of insects or chatter-
ing to each other. These smallest of North America's swallows measure only about
five inches in length and weigh less than an ounce, but they can dig themselves into a
river-side bank, excavating a den using their feet, wings, and bill. The male excavates
the burrow before he has a mate, then attracts females by flying in circles around
the burrow entrance and singing of his prowess. The male abandons the burrow if
no female chooses the site. A successful male remains paired with his mate for the
breeding season, although scientists observe both members of the pair mating with
other individuals in the colony. Despite their opportunistic mating strategies, the
numbers of bank swallows in North America have declined by a startling 89 percent
since 1970. The cause of this massive loss remains a mystery to scientists, but the
Cornell Laboratory of Ornithology lists the bank swallow as a common bird in steep
decline—not a happy state of affairs.

Most noticeable among the songbird migrants are yellow warblers. Both males
and females create flashes of vivid yellow as they move through the trees. The warblers spend the breeding season in the willow thickets growing close to the edge of
the channel. There the birds eat insects plucked from the foliage or captured during
short flights. Black-and-white warblers, striped like a sports referee, nest on the
ground and feed primarily on butterfly and moth caterpillars during their breeding
season on the Kechika. The black-and-white warbler is the only member of the genus *Mniotilta*, which means "moss-plucking" and describes the bird's habit of probing bark and moss for insects. An extra-long hind claw and heavier legs improve the
warbler's ability to grasp and move across bark. The warbler aggressively defends its
territory against other insect-eating songbirds not only when raising chicks, but also
on the wintering grounds in Central America and northern South America.

Yellow-bellied sapsuckers settling in for the breeding season prefer the soft
wood of black poplars for excavating a nest cavity. These birds feed on flying insects
such as moths and mayflies. When insects are scarce, the sapsuckers also suck the
sap of trees from rows of sap wells that the birds bore into the trunk. Their name is
one of those mysteries of bird identification, for a yellow belly is not their most obvious characteristic. If anything, they might be called crimson-crowned sapsuckers.
A bright red patch of feathers crowns both males and females, with black-and-white
facial stripes, and then another red patch on the throat for the males.

In contrast to the summer residents, snowy owls only winter along the Kechika,
moving into the High Arctic—the northern coast of Greenland and Victoria and
Banks Islands and the northern half of Baffin Island off Canada's north coast—in

summer. The large white owls prefer treeless spots and open spaces, but in winter they perch on elevated features like trees while scanning the landscape for small mammals, ptarmigans, and waterfowl.

Among the year-round residents are great horned owls, which are catholic in their habitat preferences and diet. These big owls with long, earlike tufts rising from their head eat everything from tiny rodents or insects to hares, skunks, geese, and raptors, perching until they spot prey and then swooping down to pursue the hapless animal. Common ravens are equally broad in selecting habitat and food, from carrion to buds and berries. The large black birds nest either on cliffs under a rock overhang or in a woven twig-basket high in a tree. Barred owls nest in tree cavities, including those in balsam poplars, but only when great horned owls are not too close. Great horned owls can prey on the slightly smaller barred owls, whose facial markings make them appear perennially anxious. Barred owls tend to have small territories in which they hunt for rodents, rabbits, small birds, fish, and invertebrates.

The poplar stand is also in the southern part of the willow ptarmigan's year-round range. This species of grouse has a feather wardrobe as beautiful and varied as any fashion model. Winter plumage of both sexes is white as driven snow, including thickly feathered legs that make it look as though the bird wears downy pantaloons. As the real snow melts, the females change to mottled brown-and-black plumage and the breeding males develop striking red eyebrows, a chestnut-colored head and neck, a mottled brown-and-black back, and a white belly. If anything, the chicks are even more gorgeous in their coloration. Their fluffy plumage is striped in hues of golden wheat, cinnamon, and dark chocolate reminiscent of the pelt of an ocelot or a margay. The chicks do not exactly move with a cat's fluid grace, but the outsized feet of the tiny birds carry them swiftly through the undergrowth when danger threatens.

True to their name, willow ptarmigans like shrubby willow thickets in which they forage for both vegetation and insects as food. The birds leave distinctive markers where they have eaten or roosted—cylindrical droppings that resemble tiny brown or tan sausages tightly stuffed with undigested bits of willow. When disturbed, ptarmigans usually fly only a short distance, uttering a guttural, increasingly rapid cry that sounds like *uh, uh, uh, ugh-agh-agh*.

Ruffed grouse also eat a variety of plant parts where younger forest stands are present along the river. Although the plumage of these grouse is less visually striking than that of the ptarmigan, the males put on an amazing mating display, raising a black neck ruff and handsomely striped tail, and goose-stepping on stiff legs.

Hairy woodpeckers are another year-round resident among the poplars, exca-

A male willow ptarmigan in breeding plumage, here in the Arctic tundra.

vating sizable cavities using their massive bill and strongly constructed neck. Insects make up most of the woodpecker's diet, with the larvae of wood-boring beetles and bark beetles, ants, and moth pupae being high on the list of edibles. There is no obvious reason the birds are called hairy. They might just as well be called elegant, with their black-and-white plumage like formal evening attire and the vibrant patch of red at the rear of the male's head.

In addition to the birds, the stand of poplars along the Kechika hosts a healthy population of various types of rodents, snowshoe hares, and the animals that prey on them—martens, long-legged Canada lynx, black bears, and wolverines. Mule deer, elk, moose, and caribou all live in or pass through the river corridor, as do wolves and grizzly bears. Stone sheep and mountain goats frequent the higher lands back from the channel and floodplain. Beavers build dams and ponds on the floodplain back from the main channel. Some of the poplar's neighbors are taken down by the beavers for their dams and lodges.

Time-lapse images of the river corridor would record the seasonal fluctuations: Arctic grayling, perhaps the most unusually shaped of the salmonids, with a tall dorsal fin rising from their back like a sail, laying their eggs in sand along the river's edge as melting snow begins to raise the water level. Populations of insects and migratory songbirds swelling while the deciduous trees and shrubs leaf out. Nestlings learning to fly, beaver kits exploring the world around their lodge, and fluffy goslings lengthening into sleekly feathered geese. Water levels in the river dropping as the poplar leaves turn yellow and then carpet the ground. Bull trout migrating upstream to spawn as water temperatures drop, and then each female fanning the stream bed with her muscular tail to create a depression in which to lay her eggs. Snow drifting across the frozen river and among the trees. Ptarmigans roosting in the snow during the coldest periods.

Slower changes spread across the years would appear in the maturing forest on the point bar along with irregular shifts in the position of the channel, perhaps even a fall of rocks from a river-side cliff or the collapse of a tall stream bank. Occasionally, one of the trees leaning at a perilous angle out over the channel finally falls into the water. The life of the river flows through time as the poplar gradually ages.

Death

Under the best conditions, a poplar lives at most two hundred years. By then, the floodplain on which it grows would be dominated by white spruce. The poplar of this tale never attains that age, however, because the Kechika is once more on the move. This time the river erodes along its left bank and removes the portion of floodplain in which the poplar is rooted. Over a period of a few days, the roots of the big tree come under strain and begin to tear as the weight of the trunk and crown leans toward the river and the soil around the roots is washed away by the river's flow. The tree tilts at an angle seemingly impossible to sustain. The tips of some of the longest branches on the river side, which are already partly submerged, vibrate in the current. The big tree topples into the channel during the high flows of June and begins its journey downstream.

Life after Death I: The Long River Journey

The poplar topples entire—root wad, trunk, branches, and leaves—during high snowmelt flow. The water is just deep enough to mostly float the tree and keep it moving in fits and starts downstream. The leaves are stripped relatively quickly and the smaller branches and protruding roots break off as the tree rolls and bounces down the cobble stream bed and between bars along the side of the channel. As the snowmelt peak starts to decline, the poplar grounds on a bar at the side of the channel and remains there during the following year.

Through the remainder of the summer, the clear waters of the Kechika flow over a bed of gray and white cobbles. River creatures concentrate around the partly submerged poplar. Biofilm coats the submerged portions of the poplar, and macroinvertebrates arrive to graze on the biofilm. The few remaining leaves detach from the tree and collect in eddies downstream, where they form nutritious food for shredder macroinvertebrates. Filter-feeding macroinvertebrates attach themselves to the poplar and put a silken net into the current. Stoneflies spin silk threads to attach their cases to the tree's surface.

Increasing numbers of insects and crustaceans attract fish. Tiny fish take refuge in the shallow water among the poplar branches. Arctic grayling feed on invertebrates and then linger beneath the cover of the poplar trunk and root wad. The submerged wood obstructs streamflow, creating eddies of lower velocity in which fish can rest. The complex shapes of branches and multiple pieces of wood create overhead cover from raptors, but the haven also attracts piscine predators including northern pike. The partly submerged poplar is analogous to a coral reef in the ocean—a small patch that hosts a diverse community of organisms by providing numerous habitat niches in a concentrated area.

In the cold, relatively dry climate, there is little colonization of the exposed portions of the downed tree by microbes and fungi. The bark progressively flakes off and the small branches continue to break, but most of the change occurs during the following snowmelt season when another large log slamming into the tree dislodges the poplar and sends it once more down the channel. This time, as a simpler shape minus many branches, the poplar floats farther downstream, past the junction with the much larger Liard River, more than twenty meandering river miles below the site where the poplar once grew. The name of the Liard appears to derive from a French word for the balsam poplar.

Along its course, the Kechika passes densely forested banks and many accumulations of large wood along the channel margins. Shallow riffles over bars alternate repeatedly downstream with deep pools of clear, turquoise-hued water. Bars along the river show a regular plant succession, with willow thickets closest to the water, backed by young stands of poplar, and then conifers. Many of the conifers growing close to the channel lean out over the water at more or less unsustainable angles—future converts to the population of large wood in the river. The stream banks alternate repeatedly downstream between broad, exposed cobble bars and eroding bluffs of glacial sediment and bedrock.

Once the Kechika joins the Liard, the channel remains about five hundred to six hundred feet wide but grows deeper. The floating balsam poplar log passes the big birds that seek food along the margins of big rivers: trumpeter and tundra swans as well as sandhill cranes and white pelicans, all probing the river margins for aquatic insects, small vertebrates, and plants.

On the poplar trunk goes, more than a hundred winding river miles to the junction with the Toad River, then another 120-plus river miles to Fort Liard, one of the historic fur-trading posts in the region, and yet another hundred river miles to the junction with the South Nahanni River, which takes its name from a Dene word. Beyond that, yet another 115-plus river miles, lies the junction with the great Mackenzie River.

The poplar log is like a suburban commuter leaving her home and joining an increasingly larger crowd along her route to a major city. Think of the network of creeks and rivers feeding the Mackenzie as a network of roads converging on a city. A suburban commuter cannot be completely certain when she will reach her office because of traffic jams. Similarly, the travel time of the poplar log between its home on the Kechika and its entry into the Arctic Ocean is not entirely certain.

About once every twenty to thirty years, some combination of higher flow and abundant wood temporarily stored along the islands and banks of the river during preceding years provides the trigger, and the Mackenzie experiences a massive wood flood. Thousands of floating logs jostle each other, obscuring the water surface as the Mackenzie becomes a river of flowing wood. Logs bounce apart and then surge together, pile up briefly, churn over and under in the swift current, snag along the channel margins, gouge the cobble bars, and batter the saplings along the water's

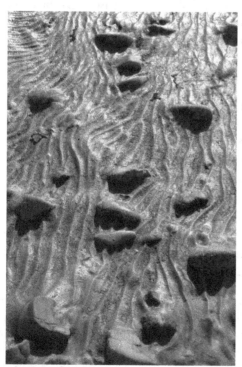

edge, but move relentlessly downstream. When the waters recede, polished drift logs pale as bones lie scattered on top of boulders that are aligned like the scales on a fish. Where silt and clay settle from the floodwaters, the cohesive sediment is sculpted into a miniature landscape of ripples and troughs that bend around protruding boulders like the raked sand of a formal Japanese garden. Logs are on the move along the Mackenzie every year, but they are like off-hour commuters. The wood floods are rush hour.

Not every log in a wood flood reaches the ocean. The commuter route is lined with off-ramps in the

Patterned sediment ripple-marked by receding flows along the banks of the river.

form of wooded islands, embayments in the riverbanks, and tributaries to the main stem. Living trees on the islands and banks can catch and hold floating wood, and other pieces of wood can drift into the backwaters of an embayment or a tributary mouth. Whole sections of wood rafts can come to rest across a large embayment, remaining there as the wood pieces trap sediment suspended in the river water, decay, and provide a germination site for new trees.

The floating poplar log does reach the ocean, but the journey takes several years. The poplar falls into the Kechika during a normal year, rather than during a wood flood, and it moves downstream for a couple of months at a time with each year's snowmelt flow before being trapped along a river edge during the intervening months or years of low flow and winter ice.

The Liard crosses over into Yukon Territory. The course of the river is complicated by numerous bars and wooded islands. During summer, cobble beaches along the river can be thick with female mergansers resting between bouts of diving for food in the waters of the cold river. Inland on one side stretch forests of thin, short, oddly knobbed black spruce trees where the ground is underlain by ice and the surface remains wet throughout the year. On the higher, drier ground across the river, the black spruces grow relatively tall and symmetrical.

In places the valley floor widens into a broad floodplain across which the channel has inscribed the looping arcs of meander bends that now host secondary channels, wetlands, and stands of differently aged forest. This is beaver paradise. Muddy slides line the banks of each secondary channel. Individual beavers move along the channel banks, cutting overhanging willow branches an inch or two in diameter and swimming each branch to a clear spot on the bank where the beaver climbs out of the water, shaking its coat like a dog. The animal quickly strips and eats the leaves and finer branches, munching loudly enough to be heard across the quietly flowing water. The broad-bodied, furry lump of the animal transforms into sleek swimming lines as the beaver again enters the water, just the top of its head and tail marking its progress. Before entering its den on the stream bank, the beaver swims in circles, scanning the surroundings. Alarms occur and loud thunks interrupt the quiet of pale summer nights when the beaver announces the situation by slamming its tail onto the water surface over and over. Many of those moving about might put the beaver on alert, for the fresh mud in the receding water lines along the channel is richly tracked by black bears, the pigeon-toed marks of grizzly bears, and wolves, as well as the more delicate lattices left by bird feet.

In places, the Liard meanders so tightly that the channel follows a path three times as long as a straight-line distance. Elsewhere, the river flows in a relatively straight path, as when it churns through the nearly twenty miles of the Grand Canyon of the Liard, where rapids called Hell Gate and Rapids of the Drowned batter and scrape the poplar log. All the bars, islands, and meanders represent places for the poplar to be hung up in its downstream journey, and, like the path of the western redcedar down the Queets, the balsam poplar's progress down the Liard is episodic. Several years pass before the poplar finally reaches the junction of the Liard and the Mackenzie River at Fort Simpson. The impetus for the final float into the Mackenzie is a year of unusually high river flow.

The Mackenzie River is named for Alexander Mackenzie. The first European to explore the river's length, Mackenzie was searching for a route to the Pacific down which furs could be shipped en route to China. He was certainly disillusioned when he reached the river's mouth and the Arctic Ocean, rather than the Pacific, in July 1789, but the story that he named it the River of Disappointment may be apocryphal.

People moved into this region as the last great ice sheet of the Pleistocene retreated some fifteen thousand years ago. The melting ice exposed new terrain for colonization, and intrepid pioneers of all types moved in: soil microbes, plants, fish, birds, mammals, and eventually waves of people—Athabaskans, Inuit, and finally Europeans bringing their diseases and their endless thirst for resources. Still, the region remains human-empty by world standards. This is a land of water in lakes, rivers, clouds, and rain, and the space through which the water moves. Widely scattered small towns like Fort Simpson only reinforce the impression of a landscape barely marked by humans.

Fort Simpson reflects the history of European presence in the Mackenzie drainage basin. Founded in 1803 as a fur trading post known as Fort of the Forks, the post was enlarged in 1822 by the Hudson's Bay Company and named for George Simpson. Simpson was the governor of the Rupert's Land territory of British North America, which encompassed the entire drainage basin of Hudson Bay. Today, about 1,200 individuals, mostly Dene and Métis people, live in the town of Fort Simpson.

Despite the large volume of water continually flowing by Fort Simpson, it is a cool, dry spot. Average snowfall is seventy-four inches, but average yearly precipitation is only fifteen inches, for the snow is dry and powdery. The air temperature has reached 98°F in July, but the average high temperature in July is a pleasant 75°F and the average low temperature in January is −19°F, with a bone-chilling recorded low of −69°F. Those winter temperatures explain the thick, rich furs that first drew Europeans to this region. Once wearing fur became less common, the few Europeans who stayed in the area clustered into small communities focused on spreading Christianity or on exploiting resources such as oil and gas.

After the junction with the Liard, the Mackenzie widens to nearly a mile. The channel still has bars, islands, and secondary channels in which to detain floating wood, but the pathway downstream is clearer and the poplar moves more swiftly. The surface of the muddy brown water is opaque and inscrutable, rising in silent boils. Where the river flows quietly, only a big moose working hard against the current, his shoulders periodically surging above the water forming an angle about him, provides a sense of how swiftly the current moves. Forests spread unbroken along both banks, growing from a thick layer of silt and clay above a band of cobbles and boulders that in places are aligned as precisely as a cobblestone pavement. Delicate, pale green or yellow insects freshly hatched from the river land briefly on the floating poplar, and dragonflies stitch back and forth through the air over the river. A bald eagle sits watching with an impassive glare as the log passes and a small black bear, darker than the heaviest shadow, appears briefly at the forest edge.

Beyond the riverbank stretches a pockmarked terrain of irregularly shaped ponds and lakes that, when seen from the air, resemble the scraps left behind by a cookie cutter. Tortuously sinuous smaller rivers wind among the lakes, leaving abandoned horseshoe-shaped bends. The soggy, sodden landscape is patterned in shades of gray and green that from above resemble patches of different mosses on a log.

Time and collisions have now whittled the complex trunk and branches of the poplar to a simple, gradually tapering cylinder with a flared base that represents the remnants of the once-complex root wad. The bark has been completely stripped and the trunk is a polished, gleaming white. Now the poplar is driftwood, still impressive in size compared to a human, yet dwarfed by the big river down which it moves.

The poplar driftwood has joined a long and famous procession of wood down the Liard and Mackenzie Rivers. The Mackenzie is renowned for pumping huge quantities of driftwood into the Arctic Ocean. Although the Mackenzie drainage includes numerous tributaries that can collect driftwood over a broad expanse of the southern headwaters, any wood floating down southern tributaries into Great Slave Lake, upstream from the poplar's path, remains in the lake.

The Slave River, in particular, episodically experiences wood floods that fill its 1,600–6,500-foot-wide channel with floating logs. When the wood enters the 10,500 square miles of Great Slave Lake, winds and waves wash the logs onto the shoreline around the southern margins of the lake. On calm summer days, the placid lake surface is blue satin at midday and reflects bands of fire as the sun sets. In winter, blasting winds can drive thick cakes of ice grinding against the shoreline.

In the upper image, recently deposited driftwood berm on the rocky shore of Great Slave Lake. Seedlings and saplings are just beginning to grow among this driftwood. Farther back from the shore, to the right, mature conifers grown on older driftwood berms. In the lower image, large wood temporarily stored on the low bedrock islands that form the Slave River Rapids, just upstream from the river's junction with Great Slave Lake.

Along steep sections of shore, each winter's big storms pile the wood up in berms on the cobble beach between the lake water and the forest. The berms trap sediment and plant seeds and the forest grows over these berms and moves beyond them toward the lake. With time, the lakeshore forest assumes a banded appearance, with lines of trees established on old berms parallel to the water's edge. On more gently sloping shorelines, the driftwood accumulates in mats. The collection of driftwood as berms or mats helps form complexly shaped shorelines that increase the abundance and diversity of habitat for creatures from aquatic insects and fish to birds and mammals. The partly floating, partly vegetated mats of driftwood also buffer the shoreline against erosion by ice and waves.

Given the wood-trapping abilities of Great Slave Lake, the driftwood for which the Mackenzie is famous originates mostly in the Liard River catchment. Written descriptions of the Mackenzie driftwood date to at least 1921, but driftwood coming down the river and redistributed by the East Greenland Current in the Arctic Ocean has traditionally been an important resource for Inuit living in Greenland.

Indigenous people along the river network of the Mackenzie and throughout the Arctic coastal communities put driftwood to many uses. Fish could be trapped and then speared in structures built of rock and driftwood in the river shallows. Along the coasts, driftwood traditionally provided fuel for fires, building materials for semisubterranean houses constructed of wood and sod, kayak and umiak frames, and portions of weapons, tools, and utensils. So important was driftwood that anthropologists describe people singing and dancing for the return of the driftwood in spring, just as they did for seals or salmon. Knowledge of driftwood accumulation sites was as highly valued as knowledge of good hunting or fishing sites.

For nearly the first hundred miles downstream from the junction, the turbid brown waters of the snowmelt-peak Liard are clearly distinguishable in satellite imagery from the green waters of the Mackenzie. Beyond this lengthy mixing zone, water in the Mackenzie is all one color. A broad riparian fringe of bright green shrubby willow, mature willow, and then aspen lines both sides of the channel, giving way to spruce farther from the banks. Beyond the banks, from here to the ocean, millions of ponds and lakes feed the infamous abundance of Arctic mosquitoes. These numerous wetlands persist despite the dry climate because they are underlain by permanently frozen ground that prevents rainfall and snowmelt from infiltrating very far. The center of the broad main channel is sufficiently breezy that it provides one of the few places in this landscape to escape the summer hordes of voracious mosquitoes.

Along the banks of the Mackenzie. Driftwood lies parallel to the bank among sapling willows, with mature willows and aspen farther from the shoreline. Conifers are present farther back from the channel.

From a relatively simple, single channel at Fort Simpson, the Mackenzie downstream splits into secondary channels around wooded islands, like a braided rope starting to unravel. The subdued topography left after the Laurentide Ice Sheet planed the ancient rocks of the Canadian Shield surrounds the river to the junction with the tributary North Nahanni River. As flow in the river declines during late summer, the poplar log beaches at the head of one of these small islands. And there the log remains, frozen into the ice, through the long darkness of a subarctic winter.

With the coming of spring, the uppermost rivers in the Mackenzie drainage basin thaw first, for they lie far to the south, in warmer climes. Ice-jam breakout floods are common along the northward-flowing Mackenzie. Thawing rivers in the southern headwaters send down a steadily increasing volume of flow that stresses and then fractures the thick ice of the lower rivers. Like a wood flood, an ice-jam breakout flood is a forceful surge of solid chunks—in this case ice cakes that can be tens of feet across. Blocks of ice gouge and pit the cobble banks of the river, batter the river-side trees, and pile up in temporary ice dams that send water spilling across the floodplain. The winter hiatus of the poplar log's journey is abruptly ended as surging ice rips up the log and carries it once more downstream.

Mountains form the horizon of the riverscape.

The Mackenzie Mountains appear on the western horizon past the North Nahanni junction as the river and the poplar log pass through Camsell Bend, named for Julian Camsell. Having started as a clerk with the Hudson's Bay Company in 1859, Camsell became the first mercantile agent of the combined Northwest and Hudson's Bay Company in 1884. At the bend, the Mackenzie shifts from a west-north-west to a more northerly course. In places, the vegetation on the mountains is so sparse that the slopes resemble an enormous badland.

Past the junction with the tributary Root River, the Mackenzie slims back down to a single channel. A cabin built in a clearing sits on a terrace next to the mouth of many of the smaller tributary creeks that enter the river. Driftwood accumulates on broad, shallow sandbars when floodwaters recede. By late summer during most years, at least some part of the horizon is smudged with smoke from slow-burning, lightning-generated fires that are allowed to burn out unless they threaten one of the few, widely scattered towns in the area.

As the floating log approaches the town of Wrigley, the Franklin Mountains appear on the eastern horizon and the topography on the western side of the river corridor becomes rumpled. Like Fort Simpson, founded in 1803 as a fur trading site, Wrigley derives from the era of the fur trade. Originally located ten miles downstream and named Fort Wrigley after Joseph Wrigley, an official in

A slowly burning wildfire along the banks of the Mackenzie, seen on an August day of low clouds and steady rain. Driftwood at the base of the conifers reflects high flows along the river.

the Hudson's Bay Company, Wrigley relocated during World War II to host a regional airport.

Past the junctions with the Johnson, the Blackwater, the Dahadinni, and the Redstone Rivers, the Mackenzie remains slender but for the occasional wooded island around which the channel widens like the body of a snake containing an undigested animal. At intervals, large, slumping banks beside the channel bristle with trees tilted at all angles, slowly moving toward their future as driftwood. Some of the steep banks contain seams of coal burning so slowly that they remain as Alexander Mackenzie described them in the late eighteenth century. The heat of the fire has baked the surrounding sediment to a bright orange hue.

The floating poplar log approaches a flock of scoters tightly clustered on the water surface. The birds take flight in a precise line low over the water, their white wing bars flashing a diamond pattern against their black plumage. A raven peering from a hole in a high cutbank watches the log and the scoters.

Beyond the Redstone junction the river again splits into multiple, more or less parallel channels, continuing beyond the Keele River junction, the town of Tulita (formerly Fort Norman and the site of another Hudson's Bay Company trading post), and the junction where the Great Bear River contributes its robin's-egg-blue waters. The poplar log floats past the town of Norman Wells, where mountains rise at a distance on both sides of the river. An ancient coral reef that formed four hun-

An extensive portion of bank is slowly slumping into the Mackenzie River, taking a portion of forest with it.

dred million years ago lies some six hundred feet below the channel here, and an array of wells pump oil from the carbonate rocks of the former reef. Natural gas being flared and burned from the wells lights the area along the river day and night.

Downstream, the Carcajou River enters slender and sinuous, then the Mountain River braided around numerous sandbars. The Mackenzie passes through the Sans Sault Rapids and leaves behind the remaining mountains on the western horizon, flowing once more into subdued topography as the river returns to a single channel with a few wooded islands. The drifting poplar log continues past the town of Fort Good Hope, established in 1805 as a fur trading post of the Northwest Company. Just upstream from the town, the Mackenzie narrows from more than two and a half miles wide to just over 1,600 feet as the river passes the 130-foot-tall limestone cliffs

Approaching Tulita on a day of low clouds.

Pale limestone cliffs line the river channel in the Ramparts.

of the Ramparts. Here the undulating surface of the rock has weathered into shades of pale gray, buff, gold, orange, and even sulfur yellow.

Fort Good Hope's traditional name is Radeyilikoe in the language of the Sahtu Dene, signifying "where the rapids are." The town sprawls across the bluffs above the river and in summer the pickup trucks moving around the unpaved streets coat the vegetation with dust. Some of these pickup trucks are still used to haul driftwood from the river's edge, for the weathered, dried wood remains useful even in a petroleum-based lifestyle.

The Mackenzie crosses the Arctic Circle, then continues past the Gwich'in community of Tsiigehtchic (signifying "mouth of the iron river") on the mouth of the Arctic Red River. Here the river flows through a horizontal landscape—an immensity of sky and water, with a thin line of vegetation at the horizon. The deciduous trees become more sparse and black spruce dominates the forests adjacent to the channel. Black spruce is uniquely suited to the continuously frozen soil just below the surface. The spreading lateral roots of the tree allow it to grow to maturity where the seasonally thawed layer of soil is only eighteen inches deep. Conditions are challenging, though, and this slow-growing spruce species seldom exceeds a height of fifty feet.

The delta starts about fifteen river miles downstream from Tsiigehtchic, and the character of the Mackenzie changes substantially in the final 170 river miles to

Permafrost exposed as pale layers of ice in a cutbank along the Mackenzie River (*upper*). As river movement exposes the permafrost to warm air, the entire bank topples and recruits large numbers of trees to the river channel (*lower*).

the coastline of the Arctic Ocean. The main channel splits and then begins to break up into dozens of distributary channels that in places double back on themselves as they wind downstream in bends so tight that from the air the delta appears to have rivery varicose veins. A distinct main channel continues downstream past the town of Inuvik until, in the last fifty river miles, it becomes an arbitrary choice which channel represents the main stem. Along each of its many distributary channels, the Mackenzie steadily thaws the frozen ground in the riverbanks, exposing and eroding lenses of subterranean ice and dumping trees still green into the cold, swift-flowing water.

Some of the distributaries rejoin other channels downstream, creating a watery mesh; others remain independent entities out to the coastline. Each is interrupted by lakes and scored along the margins by irregular embayments. All these secondary channels, lakes, and embayments represent potential traps for driftwood.

Fly over the delta and the nearby coastline west of Tuktoyaktuk at an altitude of twenty thousand feet or so in Google Earth. Notice the swaths of pale tan to gray that line many of the lakes and embayments. Bands of pale tan also stripe portions of the coast east and west of the Mackenzie's mouth, from the town of Tuktoyaktuk west to Herschel Island. Then swoop down to a lower elevation. This closer view reveals that the apparently sandy beaches forming the pale swaths are actually thick mats of logs scraped clean of bark, whittled to a single tapering cylinder, and bleached to a uniform pale tan. Southwest of Tuktoyaktuk, for example, the ice-cored mound of a pingo rises like a volcanic cone from a broad coastal embayment where a raft of driftwood half a mile long and three hundred to four hundred feet wide lines the inner shores of the embayment (location 69.39976° N, 133.07884° W). A mile to the west, another embayment is lined with a driftwood mat nearly a thousand feet long on each side.

Even more beached driftwood lies hidden from view. On the ground, close examination reveals that the bands of shrubby willows growing parallel to the river channels are rooted in partly decayed berms of driftwood. More obvious are the bleached white lines of driftwood above the channel edges that mark the high water of the most recent flood.

The poplar of our tale hits hard against a tree leaning over the channel's edge, and a large portion of the upper trunk of the poplar breaks off. The broken top floats into an embayment about halfway down the delta. There it remains for centuries.

The poplar piece is one of thousands stored in the embayment. All have been abraded to a smooth finish, and the bleached, tan wood resembles the drying bones of a huge animal. The wood pieces arrange themselves parallel to one another and

Driftwood accumulating in a wood-mat in an embayment along the Mackenzie Delta. An ice-cored hill known as a pingo rises on the horizon at right.

to the edge of the shore in the embayment. As more pieces are added through time, the area covered by the wood mat grows.

Pieces in storage the longest begin to flake, peel, and crack, as rain or snow wets them and ice expands in the cracks and then melts again. Fine sediment settles under the wood and seeds blow onto it. Gradually, the wood at the back is incorporated into the river shoreline. Rodents move into the stable, dry portions of the wood mat and weasels come to hunt them.

In the cold, dry Arctic climate, the wood undergoes remarkably little chemical change, and all the processes of decay and decomposition undergone by the Engelmann spruce and the western redcedar are essentially absent as long as the driftwood remains exposed at the surface. Only once it is completely buried and pioneering vegetation such as shrubby willows grows over it do soil microbes and fungi begin to slowly, slowly break down the wood.

In the past, even burial might not have resulted in complete decay if the wood was frozen into the permafrost. Now, under a warming climate, thawing permafrost is reexposing buried and frozen wood that can be tens of thousands of years old. The warmer the air and the soil become, the happier are the microbes that feast on carbon and other nutrients formerly frozen into the soil. Arctic rivers

Details of pieces of driftwood about a foot in length, abraded and polished en route to deposition in the delta (*upper*). Some of the wood fragments to inch-long pieces that create a wood beach among the larger driftwood pieces (*lower*).

An abandoned channel on the Mackenzie Delta, now filled with driftwood that is being slowly colonized and hidden by willows.

are now experiencing microbial blooms as the soil along stream banks thaws and slumps into the river, providing bountiful nutrients for river microbial communities. One of the unfortunate by-products of this process is the emission of carbon dioxide to the air, which contributes to the greenhouse warming that is driving warmer climates.

By releasing greenhouse gases that thaw more permafrost and release more nutrients, the microbes are helping to enhance their own food supply, but they cannot consume everything released by the thawing soils to the rivers. Measurements taken during the past few decades indicate greater quantities of freshwater and nutrients flowing into the Arctic Ocean.

Permafrost along Arctic coastlines is also thawing, causing slumping of coastal cliffs and rapid coastal erosion that further increase the sediment and nutrients entering the ocean. This is not a minor, local problem. A third of Earth's coastline occurs in permafrost zones of the Arctic. The amount of carbon being released by these eroding coastlines equals the amount being released by all the great rivers of the Arctic. Combined with the rapid loss of winter ice cover in the ocean, these changes are triggering shifts in Arctic marine ecosystems.

Nearshore coastal organisms depend on the nutrients coming in via river discharge and coastal erosion. These nutrients fuel food webs of invertebrates that feed fish, which are in turn critical to the subsistence lifestyles of Arctic native people. Carbon coming from eroding soil and vegetation may supply up to half the total carbon needed by fish that regularly migrate between Arctic rivers and the ocean. As more carbon enters nearshore areas from river runoff and coastal erosion, it can follow different paths. Some can enter the atmosphere as greenhouse-inducing carbon dioxide. Some can fuel population increases of marine organisms. Carbon can also be buried in nearshore sediments or be transported offshore. We do not yet know which paths the extra carbon will follow, but, like the traveler in Robert Frost's poem "The Road Not Taken," the paths will make all the difference to atmospheric carbon dioxide levels and our warming climate.

Meanwhile, the larger piece of the original poplar trunk keeps floating through the delta to the shores of the Arctic Ocean. Some of the wood traveling with the poplar eddies out onto the sandy beaches along the coast. That driftwood helps stabilize windblown sand and provide habitat for diverse plants and animals, as happens with the western redcedar. The poplar, however, keeps going into the open ocean.

Life after Death II: The Arctic Ocean

An estimated eighty-one cubic miles of water flows from the Mackenzie each year. That number is a little hard to visualize, but it's about a tenth the volume of the Grand Canyon, or six hundred times as large as Sydney Harbour in Australia. However you choose to think about it, this is the greatest flow of any Arctic river in North America, although it is exceeded by volumes flowing from the Lena, Yenisei, and Ob Rivers in Siberia. As the river flow and driftwood leave the mouth of the Mackenzie, the poplar is caught up in the Beaufort Gyre, one of the two major ocean currents in the Arctic Ocean. The gyre circles clockwise off the northeastern coast of Alaska, the Canadian Arctic Archipelago, and Greenland. The poplar log is frozen into the ice pack over winter and carried in the gyre westward past the northern coast of Alaska and then along the coast of Siberia. From the gyre, the log is then carried into the Transpolar Drift, a straighter current that flows south past the northeastern coast of Greenland through the Fram Strait between Greenland and Svalbard, and into the North Atlantic.

In the past, some of the ice circled for years in the Beaufort Gyre, gradually thickening with age. Old ice that escaped the gyre was replenished with new ice growth each winter. Walt Meier of the National Snow and Ice Data Center described the former condition of the Beaufort Sea as a nursery for the development of old ice.

Now, though, the Beaufort has become a graveyard for older ice as warming climate results in ice that is more broken up and scattered, and therefore escapes the gyre more easily. Old ice is bright white, as well as thick. Satellite images reveal that this old white ice has virtually disappeared from the Arctic Ocean, which now hosts only younger, thinner, more transparent ice.

As the poplar log follows its newly hastened path from the Beaufort Sea into the Transpolar Drift, the wood starts to change. Marine bivalve mollusks known as shipworms bore into the wood. Fungi enter and begin to decompose the cellulose and lignin in the wood. About 530 species of higher marine fungi have been identified around the world. Although the general rule of thumb for species diversity is that the greatest number of species is found in the tropics and the fewest in the Arctic, one study of Arctic driftwood samples found more than a hundred different kinds of fungi in the wood. This suggests that scientists have not come close to completely cataloging all the species of marine fungi present in the world's oceans.

Like fungi in any other environment, marine fungi are picky. Different fungal communities colonize coniferous and deciduous logs. Fungal communities in driftwood also differ across the Arctic. The species within these communities suggest that some of the fungi colonizing the poplar log entered the wood way back on the Kechika. Other fungi colonized the wood during its resting stages along the Mackenzie. They all came along for the ride, and microscopic fungal filaments known as hyphae (from the Greek *huphe*, "web") now penetrate the cells of the driftwood log. If these fungi were sentient, they might be a bit surprised at the vagaries of time and chance that brought them from the boreal forest to the drift ice of the Arctic Ocean. Despite the drastic change in their environment, the fungi continue to live in the driftwood and play a key role in the nutrient cycling and food-web dynamics of the Arctic Ocean.

Bacterial soft rot is the most common form of wood decay in Arctic driftwood. Multiple species of bacteria can use special enzymes to turn patches of wood into a liquefied mush that allows the bacteria to consume the nutrients within the wood cells. This form of decay is localized, however, and much of the poplar piece remains intact.

Over the course of its life, the balsam poplar belonged to multiple communities. First there was the cohort of seedlings and saplings that matured into a forest stand capable of hosting cavity-nesting birds. Then the poplar joined the aquatic community of microbes, insects, and fish as the fallen tree moved down the Kechika and continued its long journey to the ocean. As it moved through the Beaufort Gyre and the Transpolar Drift, the poplar became part of a global community of driftwood in the oceans. During the past two decades, scientists have documented the immense importance of driftwood to marine organisms.

South of the Arctic Ocean and the poplar log, tuna and many other types of open-ocean fish tend to concentrate around large pieces of floating wood. Scientists spying on these fish find that the wood provides one-stop shopping for fish—safety, food, and cleaning. When a predator approaches, prey species crowd together under the wood, and most predators seem unable to find a victim among the crowd. Fish that come to the wood for food in the form of plankton or fungi need to be wary, however, for those that concentrate around the wood but do not take shelter under it can themselves become food for predators. Cleaning is provided by fish species that specialize in removing external parasites from other fish. Fish with parasites congregate around the wood to have themselves cleaned and also chafe against the wood, which may remove other parasites.

At lower latitudes, driftwood can raft stones into the open ocean and drop them into the fine sediments of the deep sea, puzzling future geologists. When the widely spreading roots of a rain-forest giant are ripped out by a landslide, much of the soil and rock in which the tree was rooted comes along. If a flood carries the tree and the rocks grasped by its roots out to sea, the tree can drift far across the ocean before the roots rot sufficiently to release the stones.

At all latitudes, driftwood can raft beetles and marine snails that live within wood into and across oceans to islands. The wood may even provide a link between shallow-water environments and the deep sea. This idea has been called the stepping-stones hypothesis, but stepping-logs seems more fitting.

Examination of driftwood in Papua New Guinea revealed that snails common in estuaries, which presumably like water slightly less saline than seawater, can nonetheless survive on driftwood in seawater for extended periods. This endurance allows the snails to be transported several miles to a fully marine shore. Even more surprising, these supposedly nonmarine snails are present on sunken pieces of wood at depths of more than four hundred feet in the South Pacific. The snails appear to be able to disperse as either bottom-dwelling adults or eggs. This could help explain how the organisms living in sunken-wood communities in widely scattered areas of the deep sea reached these seemingly inaccessible habitats. The presence of driftwood organisms on sunken wood from great depths indicates a remarkable ability to tolerate extreme changes in pressure, salinity, and temperature.

Mollusks such as snails are the most abundant organisms living on sunken wood in the ocean, but crustaceans also abound. Among these crustaceans are porcelain crabs and some types of squat lobsters. The latter are aptly named, flattened crustaceans that carry their relatively long tail curled beneath their body. Porcelain crabs, which are only about half an inch wide, also have a flattened body adapted for living in crevices. And, just to be confusing, they are decapod crustaceans rather than true crabs. Regardless of what's in a name, these deep-sea crustaceans use wood and its covering biofilm as their two main sources of food. They are able to eat wood because the microflora living in their gut includes bacteria and fungi that can digest wood fragments.

It is difficult to conceive of the immense distances between these relatively small patches of sunken wood. These are both horizontal and vertical distances, from the ocean surface to the abyssal plains that may lie ten thousand to twenty thousand feet beneath the water surface and experience temperatures that hover around freezing and pressures that are two hundred to six hundred times those found at sea level. Scientists did not even discover deep-sea communities until the late 1970s, and one of the many intriguing questions about these organisms is how they managed to reach their hidden ecosystem.

The relatively late discovery of deep-sea communities reflects the difficulties for humans trying to reach the abyssal depths in specially designed vehicles, or the difficulties of sending remote vehicles down to obtain images. All the studies published on deep-sea wood come from lower latitudes than the Arctic, even though several studies have documented extensive driftwood in the Arctic Ocean. At this point, we simply don't know what wood might be falling to the floor of the high-latitude seas and what creatures might be living in that wood. So, the poplar log does not contribute to the wood falls, but the sunken wood islands are so fascinating that they are worth a diversion in this story.

Wood That Sinks in the Sea

Studies of wood-boring animals suggest that sunken wood islands could provide colonization steps for deep-sea animals living at hydrothermal vents. The discovery of deep-sea organisms that could live without photosynthesis around vents on the ocean floor was a revelation. After all, photosynthesis is the critical conversion of matter to energy that directly or indirectly powers much of the life on Earth. Realizing that deep-sea animals could entirely circumvent photosynthesis was as much a surprise as it would be to find a completely different organization for living creatures on Mars.

Organisms at hydrothermal vents have evolved the remarkable ability to use the energy stored in hydrogen sulfide. These so-called chemosynthetic animals entirely bypass the normal food web that starts with photosynthesis. Instead, creatures at deep-sea vents obtain their nutrients from the superheated, mineral-rich water surging from Earth's interior into the overlying seawater. The bacteria, blind shrimp, giant white crabs, and tube worms occupying the so-called black smokers and areas around the vents seem like creatures from science fiction.

Some of the same microflora—bacteria and microscopic algae and fungi—inhabit sunken wood and hydrothermal vents. Some of the macrofauna (over a tenth of an inch) are also closely related. It's clear that sunken wood and other organic windfalls such as sunken whale carcasses provide concentrated food sources. The presence of the same species on sunken wood and hydrothermal vents suggests that sunken wood can also provide stepping-stones from the surface all the way to the seafloor: the micro- and macroflora raining down with the sinking wood seem to be able to adapt and evolve into the unique organisms that live off hydrogen sulfide at vents.

An equally fascinating and biologically diverse community of organisms inhabits portions of the seafloor where sunken wood is present. Scientists studying dredged specimens during the 1872–1876 HMS *Challenger* Expedition first recognized the existence of these sunken-wood communities. The so-called wood fall of driftwood that becomes sufficiently decayed and waterlogged to sink to the ocean floor effectively creates an oasis of food and habitat in what has been described as the barren desert abyss of the ocean, analogous to the biological oasis of a reef in the open ocean.

Wood continually enters the oceans with river water, but relatively brief massive inputs, such as those resulting from typhoons in the tropical latitudes or wood floods on the Mackenzie, create a bonanza for coastal and deep-sea environments. Waterlogged wood that sinks to the ocean floor represents a gift to deep-sea organisms: a solid chunk of organic carbon and nutrients, as well as a new habitat. Sunken wood harbors distinct and specialized communities, and repeated introduction of newly sunken wood likely helps maintain and disperse organisms in the deep sea.

Logs at the sea surface contain oxygen within tiny cavities in the wood tissue. Once wood sinks to the seafloor, sustained decay of major components such as cellulose and lignin can make the wood anaerobic (no oxygen). This absence of oxygen limits the types of organisms that can survive and decompose the wood. Cellulose is the most abundant material and can be degraded only by fungi and bacteria. Free-living microorganisms in the wood matrix facilitate decay.

Then there are the bacterial hitchhikers that come in with wood-boring bivalves, which use the wood matrix for both shelter and food. Bivalves bore into the wood using their shell and ingest the resulting wood particles, in the process creating microniches within the wood matrix for other organisms. The bivalves fill their burrows with pellets of feces mixed with mucus. In the spirit of "smaller still, ad infinitum," sunken wood hosts distinct microbial communities on the wood, in the fecal pellets of the bivalves, and in the gills of the bivalves. In this, the sunken wood is analogous to the decaying wood on a floodplain. Larger animals start to physically fragment the wood, and this provides entry points for successively smaller creatures, some of which carry the most minute organisms attached on or within their bodies. These minute organisms leave the host animal and move into the wood, and by the end, only the most resistant portions of the wood remain.

Fundamentally, the wood's cellulose stores a significant amount of energy. Some organisms have evolved mechanisms to degrade the cellulose and access this energy. In the process, these organisms create chemical compounds that can be used by other animals such as mussels, limpets, tube worms, peanut worms, and beard worms, as well as the microbial communities within the bodies of these animals. Eventually, compounds derived from the sunken wood can pass through an impressive array of creatures, fueling the diverse communities of the seafloor.

Lignin is difficult to degrade and can maintain the structure of the wood even when other components fall apart, allowing sunken logs to persist. Decomposition proceeds in stages. First, soft rot fungi and hydrolytic bacteria produce sugars such as glucose. Other bacteria and microorganisms then ferment these compounds to organic acids, carbon dioxide, and hydrogen gas. Sulfate-reducing bacteria use the hydrogen gas, leading to an enrichment of hydrogen sulfide at the surface of the wood. Other microorganisms in turn use the hydrogen sulfide by-products of wood degradation as an energy source. Whether at the top of the forest canopy or the bottom of the ocean, the diversity of microbes living in wood increases with time.

How do these organisms even find sunken wood? Such wood does tend to be concentrated in certain areas, such as estuaries and submarine canyons, but wood is also present—and colonized by organisms—on other parts of the ocean floor. Wood-eating organisms need to be swift, mobile, and abundant (dispensable) to ensure that at least some of them find their far-flung food. They tend to grow rapidly and reproduce early and in large numbers. Many of them fail and die, but swift growth and large numbers help ensure that a few survivors locate and colonize the rare and relatively short-lived habitat of deep-sea wood. Not every marine organism seeking wood lives in the fast lane, though. Some, such as peanut worms, have floating, drifting larvae that can stay larvae for up to a year, increasing their chance of finding suitable habitat sometime during that relatively long period. The adult worms can then live more than twenty years.

Other creatures then find the organisms that have found the sunken wood. Hagfish living off New Zealand, for example, eat bottom-dwelling invertebrates. The chemical composition of hagfish tissues indicates that their invertebrate prey is fed by carbon from organisms feeding on terrestrial organic matter such as wood and decaying leaves.

Drifting logs entering the ocean are a sort of Johnny Appleseed for bottom-dwelling marine environments. The logs carry with them freshwater and estuarine species. Some of these species are sufficiently adaptable to survive the enormous changes in pressure, temperature, and nutrient sources that occur as the logs sink to the seafloor. These adaptable survivors may have seeded the communities living on sunken wood islands and even the black smokers at deep-sea hydrothermal vents. The sunken logs represent deep-sea treasure chests of habitat and nutrients, and they attract invertebrates drifting or swimming through the vast spaces of the ocean, creating a community of diverse creatures surrounded by largely cold, dark water empty of life. The poplar log of this tale is probably not sufficiently dense to contribute to the deep-sea wood falls, but some of the conifer driftwood pieces entering the Arctic Ocean with the poplar may well end their journeys deep in the northern seas.

Damming the Wood Falls

Writing of life in the deep sea, marine biologists describe wood falls as huge, unexpected food sources on the ocean floor that may be fundamental in providing nutrients to these mysterious ecosystems. No one has measured how much wood lies in the abysses of the world's oceans. The vast Pacific, the stormy Atlantic, and the frigid Arctic are all too sprawling, too deep to be known and mapped in the detailed manner that we now map land surfaces. Scientists have discovered some of the wood falls, almost by accident, but we have no knowledge of their distribution across the seafloor.

Scientists do not even know how much wood enters the oceans each year when rivers flood. A single extreme storm—a cyclone, an intense convective storm, or a derecho or tornado—can rip up huge numbers of trees. If these downed trees are carried into rivers by landslides or erosion of the riverbanks along which the trees grow, an impressive quantity of wood can be carried to the ocean. In August 2009, heavy rainfall traveling across Taiwan with Typhoon Morakot saturated hillslopes on the mountainous island. Landslides carried uprooted trees into flooding rivers and the rivers sent the trees on to the Pacific. The surface of each reservoir along the course of a river with landslides was completely covered by floating wood after the typhoon. Despite these interruptions of the flow to the ocean, somewhere between ten billion and twenty billion pounds of wood entered the sea after Morakot.

Trying to understand such enormous quantities is a little like talking about the US national debt, but twenty billion pounds is about equal to ten times the weight of the Golden Gate Bridge or twenty times the weight of the Empire State Building (or three hundred times the weight of the Statue of Liberty). This from a single typhoon over a landmass covering just under fourteen thousand square miles, which is about one-quarter of the size of New York State.

The distance from hillslope forest to nearest ocean is relatively short on Taiwan, at least compared to regions like the interior of a major continent, which facilitates transport of downed trees to the ocean. Nevertheless, natural coastlines around the world have impressive accumulations of driftwood. Historic descriptions of natural wood rafts moving down the Mississippi toward the Gulf of Mexico indicate that great rivers and ocean currents can carry wood long distances from inland forests. Once wood is in the ocean, there is little to stop it. Driftwood logs from Oregon float ashore in the Marshall Islands, and logs from the Chilean coast reach French Polynesia.

Less wood reaches the oceans today than in the historical past. Deforestation has reduced global forest extent to about half of what was present before the development of agriculture, which started nearly twelve thousand years ago in parts of the world. Most rivers of the temperate latitudes are dammed, and the reservoir associated with each dam catches most or all of the large wood floating into the reservoir. The watershed of North St. Vrain Creek in which the Engelmann spruce grew provides an example. Although the headwaters are in Rocky Mountain National Park, Ralph Price Reservoir downstream from the park boundaries provides water supply for urban communities beyond the mountain front. Intense convective storms in September 2013 triggered landslides across the lower portion of the catchment, and a huge raft of floating logs collected in the reservoir. Before the reservoir was built, many of these logs would have remained in the creek or along its floodplain, but some might have eventually moved down into the South Platte River and then along the Platte, the Missouri, and the Mississippi to the Atlantic Ocean. No reservoir operator wants floating wood, however. The logs were removed from Ralph Price Reservoir, cut into smaller pieces, and destroyed.

Sometimes a dam is designed to flush accumulated wood downstream, but more commonly logs are removed and destroyed by dumping them somewhere on land, burning, wood chipping, or grinding them down into smaller pieces that can move readily downstream. The cumulative global effect of the fifty-eight thousand large dams now in existence is likely a severe reduction in wood supply to the oceans.

Indigenous peoples who at least partly maintain a subsistence lifestyle may be more aware of these changes than urban dwellers who live largely disconnected from the natural world. Archaeologist Claire Alix quotes H. Mucallum of the Shumagin Islands (Aleutians): "Driftwood is like salmon. Any place where the salmon goes to shore is a good place for wood; any place where there is driftwood is a good place for fishing." Alix then quotes Joseph Smart of Hooper Bay, Alaska, in 2003: "Long time ago all the beach used to be covered with driftwood and then today it doesn't do that anymore."

During the past two decades, we have learned some of the consequences of disrupting the supply of sediment from hillslopes to oceans. Reservoirs upstream from dams trap most of the sediment moving down a river as well as most of the wood. Globally, human activities such as deforestation and construction have increased the sediment moving within rivers by more than two billion tons per year. Trapping in reservoirs, however, has reduced the amount of sediment entering the oceans by one billion tons per year. In other words, people have significantly increased the amount of sediment coming into rivers yet decreased the sediment reaching the oceans.

Geologists speak of the sediment cascade, from weathering of bedrock on hillslopes through downslope movement into headwater streams, transport through the river network, and deposition on deltas or in shallow nearshore waters. Human activities have severely altered and disrupted this sediment cascade at every step of a sediment grain's journey. The results appear as increased erosion of riverbeds and banks, shrinking and subsidence of deltas, loss of sand beaches, and reduced supplies of vital nutrients that travel attached to particles of silt and clay. Scientists have measured alterations in sediment cascades within individual river basins and around the world, partly because many reservoir operators keep systematic records of how much sediment accumulates in the reservoir and partly because sediment moving suspended in river flow is measured in hundreds of the world's major rivers. Fewer reservoir operators record wood accumulation and removal. No one measures wood transport in rivers, yet.

Likely . . . might have . . . perhaps . . . so much uncertainty in describing wood moving into and through rivers to the oceans. We do not know how much wood entered the oceans historically. We do not know how much wood enters the oceans today. We do not know how much wood floats or sinks across the oceans, or even how much accumulates on beaches. Yet, acting within this ignorance, we continue to severely disrupt the natural flow of wood from forests to seas and in so doing create environmental changes that we do not begin to understand.

Campfire

For the balsam poplar log, the long journey from its germination site in the headwaters of the Liard, down the Liard and the Mackenzie to the Arctic Ocean, and out
into the North Atlantic, ends on the eastern coast of Greenland.

Autumn comes to the Arctic in August. Frost in the air ignites the plants of the
tundra into colors rivaling those of the deciduous forests in the northeastern United States. Autumn on the tundra, however, is a ground fire, for none of the plants
rises more than a few inches from the ground. In the wettest soil, sphagnum mosses flare into surprising colors of orange, deep pink, or maroon. Fluffy white seed
heads of Arctic cottongrass twist in the wind. On rockier ground, scarlet cranberries
shine as the rising sun melts the night's frost crystals. Dusky blue and purple berries cluster among the coppery red hues of the blueberry leaves. Crowberries black
as their namesake hang from stems that look like tiny pine branches. Pyrola leaves
remain bright green while surrounded by the crimson leaves of bearberry and bur-
gundy-hued Ross' avens. Arctic willows glow yellow as though lit from within. The
world's tiniest willows, these plants only an inch or two in height can live for more
than two hundred years, growing with agonizing slowness in the harsh conditions
of the tundra. A lone bell-shaped flower of Arctic white heather lingers into autumn.

As the grasses begin to die back, extensive networks of tunnels become more
visible. These are the work of northern collared lemmings, which remain active even
through the Arctic winter. The tunnels resemble long, narrow grooves that extend
for several feet across the surface before disappearing belowground. Lemmings are
so short and round that they look like little barrels with feet as they scurry along
their tunnels. They must keep moving to stay ahead of the hungry mouths seeking
them out, from the Arctic fox to the snowy owl and even the giant polar bear.

Autumn nights are just dim enough for the aurora borealis to appear. Some
nights a faint, diaphanous white scarf undulates slowly below the stars—lights dancing in the solar winds above our terrestrial winds. Other nights, the scarf shows hints
of red or green and moves more swiftly, arcing, spooling and unspooling, twisting,
almost like something alive. Clearly between Earth and the stars, the skeins of white
light could be a visual interpretation of a symphony, as in the animated film *Fantasia*.

Autumn on the treeless tundra also features relentless cold winds. Campfires
keep traveling humans alive, and an Inuit family harvests the driftwood poplar log
from its resting point on the gravelly beach. In the past, such gifts from the sea might
be used to carve intricate, hand-sized wooden maps of portions of the coastline of
Greenland. Today, driftwood is most likely to be reduced to campfire-sized pieces
and used during hunting expeditions. The soft, light wood of poplar is typically used

for specialized purposes such as smoking fish. Poplar is used for firewood only as a last resort in the absence of other wood that burns longer and produces more heat. The remaining portion of the balsam poplar log of this tale goes into a campfire and is almost completely consumed, releasing heat energy and contributing to a small pile of charcoal and ash that gradually releases the last of its nutrients to the alpine tundra on which the Inuit family camped.

Charcoal represents recalcitrant carbon, hard for microorganisms to degrade and consume. A few small chunks of charcoal remain after the poplar log burns. They are slightly too heavy for even the strong Arctic winds to blow away, so they remain in the charred spot created by the campfire. Windblown silt and fine sand cover the charcoal. Rain wets the spot. A seed germinates, then another. Gradually the tundra vegetation reclaims the burned spot and the charcoal fragments are buried by newly forming soil. There they will very slowly break apart into progressively smaller fragments as rootlets penetrate them and annual freezing and thawing churn the upper soil layers.

From its germination to its cremation, the poplar has provided habitat and nutrients to an almost unimaginable array of other organisms, from terrestrial lichens and cavity-nesting birds to stream invertebrates and marine fungi, bacteria, and fish. As with the Engelmann spruce and the western redcedar, the poplar has an afterlife of long duration and great value.

Conclusion: In Praise of Dead Wood

I have never created my own food. I cannot. Neither can you. All of us rely on primary producers to capture from the air, water, and soil the nutrients that we all then share in endless exchanges across time and space.

There are really only two pathways for primary producers to capture elements essential to their growth. Bacteria in hydrothermal vents in the deep ocean can convert the energy in inorganic chemical compounds to build the organic molecules found in living organisms. These bacteria can support deep-sea ecosystems that—fascinating though they are—account for only a small portion of the living organisms on Earth. Photosynthesis, in which the energy in light is used to build organic molecules, supports the majority of life. Every animal and the decomposers such as fungi rely on photosynthetic plants.

We all know this, yet it is not as simple as eating your grains, fruits, and vegetables, or eating the cow that ate vegetation. Every organism also relies on microorganisms to absorb nutrients—endophytic bacteria in the Engelmann spruce needles, ectomycorrhizal fungi in the soil, rumen microbes that help a cow digest its food, microbes in a termite's gut that allow it to digest the lignocellulose in wood, microbes in the human gastrointestinal system that defend against pathogens and help metabolize otherwise indigestible compounds in food.

Bacteria, as one type of microbe, have a bad reputation. We continually exhort each other to wash the bacteria off our hands and sterilize surfaces to remove bacteria. Less than 1 percent of the many different types of bacteria are harmful to humans, however: the great majority are beneficial and keep the living world running.

A tiny fraction of the critical roles played by different types of microbes comes out in this tale of three trees. Each tree relies on microbes for its growth and survival. Ectomycorrhizal fungi in the soil allow the tree to absorb essential nitrogen. Bacteria within the needles of the conifers, or epiphytes living on the tree branches and foliage, absorb nitrogen from the air and pass it on to the living tissues of the tree. Microbes are also crucial intermediaries in making the nutrients held within the tissues of the tree available to other organisms during the tree's lifetime and after the tree's death. Thinking about the extraordinary variety of organisms that draw sustenance from a living or dead tree creates a pointed reminder of the importance of unseen creatures. When Robert Louis Stevenson wrote, "The world is so full of a number of things, I'm sure we should all be as happy as kings," he likely was not thinking of microbes, but the sentiment applies to the world unseen by humans, too. Without microbes, neither we nor the world as we know it would exist.

Why focus on microbes at the end of a tale of three trees? Largely because of how we regard dead trees and what we do with them. Mostly, we try to remove them. We pull dead wood from rivers and lakes, drag logs off the forest floor or the sandy beach, cut trees down before they have the chance to die and fall over, chop them up, burn them. We do this because we perceive dead wood as waste, as hazard, as unsightly mess. Yet what we perceive as waste and mess is opportunity and wealth to a huge number of other living creatures and inherently vital to the interconnected diversity and functioning of life.

The more I learn about dead wood, the more I am struck by the harm caused by our obsessive human desire to control and homogenize everything, from forests to rivers to coastlines. Scientific understanding clearly indicates that removing dead wood does a great disservice to the rest of the living world.

In a forest, snags provide habitat for cavity-nesting birds, and habitat and food for invertebrates and the many organisms that eat them. Downed dead wood feeds and houses plants, fungi, invertebrates, reptiles, amphibians, birds, and mammals. The decaying wood returns nutrients and moisture to the soil and helps new trees grow.

In a river, downed wood slows the flow of water and the sediment, dissolved material, and bits of dead plants the water carries. Wood alters the form of the channel, creating backwater pools, undercut banks, and secondary channels that provide habitat for aquatic plants, invertebrates, and fish. Logjams blocking the channel send the stream flowing off across the floodplain, undercutting existing trees and toppling them into the channel, but also leaving sediment in which new trees can germinate, ultimately creating a diverse forest. Fallen trees carried to the coastline by the river represent a gift from the land to the living creatures of the coastline and the open ocean.

On a sandy beach, driftwood provides a point of stability among the constantly moving grains of sand. The wood traps moving sand and fine organic material, creating seedbeds for plants and protected, slightly moister habitats for fungi, lichens, and invertebrates. Driftwood floating on the open ocean hosts invertebrates and fungi that feed other organisms and creates a floating refuge for fish. When the wood sinks to the ocean floor, some of the surface microbes sink and survive as well and may once have provided the evolutionary seeds for deep-sea communities. Sunken wood creates biological bonanzas for microorganisms and invertebrates. Compounds dissolved from fallen trees provide nutrients that fuel river and marine creatures.

When we short-circuit all this exchange between forests, rivers, and oceans, we impoverish the biotic communities and nutrients available in each ecosystem in ways we do not yet fully understand. Maybe it makes little difference if the wood-boring bivalves of the deep sea disappear or if the sandhoppers that need driftwood vanish into extinction. I don't know, but I'm willing to bet that it will eventually make a difference. Perhaps the greatest truth demonstrated by environmental science is that the more we investigate, the stronger grows the realization that no organism can exist without its supporting web of interactions with other organisms. Most of these interactions are invisible to the human eye. John Muir famously wrote that "when we try to pick out anything by itself, we find it hitched to everything else in the Universe." That insight has stood the test of time in ways that he likely did not imagine, yet the actions of human societies almost never reflect this fundamental understanding.

I think an important part of acting in ways that reflect this understanding is to change our aesthetic and our perception of what is appropriate and attractive. A conifer forest with a clean—sterile—understory of nothing but fallen needles is easy to walk through. A river that flows straight and unobstructed is easy to paddle. A white sand beach lacking sea wrack and driftwood has a lot of sunbathing spots. However, none of these environments is as healthy as it could be and is therefore no longer as beautiful to me as the fecund messiness of a forest rich in downed, dead wood, a river flowing through and around and over logjams, or a beach adorned with lines of driftwood sculpted by rivers and waves. We do not even use words in a manner that reflects appreciation of dead wood. David Haskell noted that "our language does a poor job of recognizing this afterlife of trees."

I think back to Mark Harmon's idea of morticulture, which proposes that human societies might deliberately manage and protect dead wood as we do living trees. Morticulture could be extended well beyond forests, to the ways we think about death and dead organisms overall, including ourselves. The idea of embalming a dead person and burying the body in an ornate wooden casket infused with chemicals to prevent decay, or of cremating a body and then entombing the ashes in a concrete vault or a ceramic or steel urn goes against any understanding of humans as part of the greater web of life. To sequester a dead body in this way is to remove its nutrients from the living world for centuries to millennia and therefore to repudiate all the processes that allowed that person to thrive while living. And to burn dead wood removed from a forest floor, a river, or a beach simply for the sake of getting rid of something considered unsightly or hazardous is to repudiate the web of life on which all living organisms depend.

Although tropical rain forests in Southeast Asia and the Amazon basin continue to be cut and burned, and coral reefs continue to be overfished, there are now some restraints on these activities and protection for these environments. As scientific research has demonstrated the importance of rain forests and coral reefs, and awareness of this importance has diffused to society as a whole, constituencies have grown to protect these and other imperiled environments. When people begin to understand, they start to care and to act on their concern, and laws and behaviors slowly change. The danger is that change does not come fast enough to save the imperiled ecosystem.

One of the outgrowths of research on old-growth forests in Oregon during the 1970s and 1980s was recognition of the beneficial effects of dead wood in streams. By the end of the twentieth century, that recognition had been translated into reintroducing wood into streams from which the wood had been historically stripped. At first the reintroduction was cautious, even timid. A log here, another log there, perhaps even a small logjam, all of them cabled or staked or otherwise fastened in place. For each person trying to reintroduce wood into streams, ten others were protesting that the log would come loose and tear downstream, careening into bridges or stream banks and running amok.

Stream restoration grew into a billion-dollar industry in the United States as the many detrimental effects of engineering streams into canals became more apparent. Listing these effects calls to mind Hamlet's famous line: "The time is out of joint." The rivers and streams are out of joint, with steadily increasing flood damage, extinction rates of freshwater species that far exceed those of terrestrial organisms, loss of sediment to coastlines and widespread beach erosion, and so much nitrate in the water that massive nearshore dead zones develop wherever a major river flows from an industrialized country into the ocean.

Early stream restoration efforts emphasized stability. The stream might be bulldozed into a meandering form that appeared more natural than an arrow-straight channel. However, fixing the meanders in place with large rocks lining each stream bank prevented the continual sideways movement of each bend that characterizes a natural meandering channel. Deliberately designed channels are still fixed in place under the illusion that this restores a stream, but restoration has gradually come to emphasize connections and ongoing adjustments. This is where dead wood plays a role. Even a small, engineered logjam fixed in place is better than no wood in a forested stream.

Stream restoration in the Pacific Northwest region of the United States now mandates consideration of large wood as part of the restoration design. National guidelines for stream restoration in the United States, the United Kingdom, and the European Union include the use of large wood. Scientists with the US Forest Service in Oregon have gone much further than a single piece of wood, with more than a dozen restoration projects in which hundreds of downed trees have been re-introduced to channels, typically using heavy equipment to knock down river-side trees or helicopters to drop wood into the river. These pieces of wood are then left to rearrange themselves as floods come down the river.

These projects, which have been undertaken on rivers in national forest lands with less infrastructure and private or commercial property that might be damaged by floating logs or wood rafts, are nonetheless controversial. Some observers worry about damage from mobile logs; others think that too many logs have been dumped into the rivers. The scientists undertaking the restoration are proceeding carefully, however, and documenting the effects of reintroducing so much wood. Their work gives me hope. I think it is hard to even conceive of how much wood was once naturally present from headwater streams through to the largest rivers flowing into the oceans. Our small-scale tinkering with a few pieces of wood in this stream and a few in that stream does no harm, but neither does it do more than begin to compensate for the widespread, massive losses of wood from streams and rivers. If we want to recover from past mistakes, we need to think and act on a larger scale in the least densely populated river corridors that remain in industrialized countries.

Years ago, my colleague Karen Prestegaard proposed that those conducting river restoration should imitate physicians working under the Hippocratic Oath: first, do no harm. The humility and caution implied by this oath reflect the understanding that when we interfere in the working of a forest or a river, we always act from limited knowledge and uncertainty regarding the outcomes of our actions. I believe that we can do better as our insight into the natural world continues to expand. The amazing interconnections illustrated by the tale of three trees underscore why we need humility when working with forests, rivers, and dead wood. So, whenever you find yourself beside flowing water, consider the river *and* the trees.

The beauty of wood, living and dead, here along a subalpine stream in Colorado.

References

Of Trees and Rivers

Gibling, M. R., and N. S. Davies. 2012. Palaeozoic landscapes shaped by plant evolution. *Nature Geoscience* 5:99–105.

Harmon, M. E. 2001. Moving towards a new paradigm for woody detritus management. *Ecological Bulletins* 49:269–278.

Luoma, J. R. 2006. *The Hidden Forest: The Biography of an Ecosystem.* Corvallis: Oregon State University Press.

Montgomery, D. R., B. D. Collins, and J. M. Buffington. 2003. Geomorphic effects of wood in rivers. In *The Ecology and Management of Wood in World Rivers*, edited by S. V. Gregory, K. L. Boyer, and A. M. Gurnell, 21–47. American Fisheries Society Symposium 37. Bethesda, MD.

Wohl, E. 2014. A legacy of absence: Wood removal in US rivers. *Progress in Physical Geography* 38:637–663.

Headwaters

ENGELMANN SPRUCE, SPRUCE BEETLES, AND EPIPHYTES

Alexander, R. R., and W. D. Shepperd. 1990. *Picea engelmannii*: Engelmann spruce. In *Silvics of North America*, vol. 1, *Conifers*, edited by R. M. Burns and B. H. Honkala, 187–203. USDA Forest Service Agriculture Handbook 654. Washington, DC.

Aplet, G. H., R. D. Laven, and F. W. Smith. 1988. Patterns of community dynamics in Colorado Engelmann spruce–subalpine fir forests. *Ecology* 69:312–319.

Arthur, M. A., and T. J. Fahey. 1992. Biomass and nutrients in an Engelmann spruce–subalpine fir forest in north central Colorado: Pools, annual production, and internal cycling. *Canadian Journal of Forest Research* 22:315–325.

Arthur, M. A., and T. J. Fahey. 1993. Throughfall chemistry in an Engelmann spruce–subalpine fir forest in north central Colorado. *Canadian Journal of Forest Research* 23:738–742.

Backlund, S., M. Jonsson, J. Strengbom, A. Frisch, and G. Thor. 2016. A pine is a pine and a spruce is a spruce—the effect of tree species and stand age on epiphytic lichen communities. *PLoS ONE* 11:e0147004.

Baker, W. L., and T. T. Veblen. 1990. Spruce beetles and fires in the nineteenth-century subalpine forests of western Colorado, USA. *Arctic and Alpine Research* 22:65–80.

Campbell, J., and D. S. Coxson. 2001. Canopy microclimate and arboreal lichen loading in subalpine spruce-fir forest. *Canadian Journal of Botany* 79:537–555.

Cardoza, Y. J., J. C. Moser, K. D. Klepzig, and K. F. Raffa. 2008. Multipartite symbioses among fungi, mites, nematodes, and the spruce beetle, *Dendroctonus rufipennis*. *Environmental Entomology* 37:956–963.

Carrell, A. A., and A. C. Frank. *Pinus flexilis* and *Picea engelmannii* share a simple and consistent needle endophyte microbiota with a potential role in nitrogen fixation. *Frontiers in Microbiology* 5:333.

Eversman, S., C. M. Wetmore, K. Glew, and J. P. Bennett. 2002. Patterns of lichen diversity in Yellowstone National Park. *Bryologist* 105:27–42.

Gough, L. P. 1975. Cryptogam distributions on *Pseudotsuga menziesii* and *Abies lasiocarpa* in the Front Range, Boulder County, Colorado. *Bryologist* 78:124–145.

Hart, S. J., T. T. Veblen, K. S. Eisenhart, D. Jarvis, and D. Kulakowski. 2014. Drought induces spruce beetle (*Dendroctonus rufipennis*) outbreaks across northwestern Colorado. *Ecology* 95:930–939.

Hauck, M. 2011. Site factors controlling epiphytic lichen abundance in northern coniferous forests. *Flora* 206:81–90.

Hinds, T. E., F. G. Hawksworth, and R. W. Davidson. 1965. Beetle-killed Engelmann spruce: Its deterioration in Colorado. *Journal of Forestry* 63:536–542.

Holsten, E. H., R. Their, A. Munson, and K. Gibson. 1999. *The Spruce Beetle*. Forest Insect and Disease Leaflet 127. USDA Forest Service.

Jenkins, M. J., E. G. Hebertson, and A. S. Munson. 2014. Spruce beetle biology, ecology and management in the Rocky Mountains: An addendum to spruce beetle in the Rockies. *Forests* 5:21–71.

Jones, M. D., F. Grenon, H. Peat, M. Fitzgerald, L. Holt, L. J. Philip, and R. Bradley. 2009. Differences in 15N uptake amongst spruce seedlings colonized by three pioneer ectomycorrhizal fungi in the field. *Fungal Ecology* 2:110–120.

Knight, F. 1958. Effects of woodpeckers on populations of the Engelmann spruce beetle. *Journal of Economic Entomology* 51:603–607.

Knowles, P., and M. C. Grant. 1983. Age and size structure analyses of Engelmann spruce, ponderosa pine, lodgepole pine, and limber pine in Colorado. *Ecology* 64:1–9.

Kulakowski, D., T. T. Veblen, and P. Bebi. 2003. Effects of fire and spruce beetle outbreak legacies on the disturbance regime of a subalpine forest in Colorado. *Journal of Biogeography* 30:1445–1456.

Lynch, A. M., and T. W. Swetnam. 1992. Old-growth mixed-conifer and western spruce budworm in the Southern Rocky Mountains. In *Old-Growth Forests in the Southwest and Rocky Mountain Regions: Proceedings of a Workshop*, edited by M. R. Kaufmann, 66–80. USDA Forest Service General Technical Report RM-213. Fort Collins, CO.

Reynolds, K. M., and E. H. Holsten. 1994. Relative importance of risk factors for spruce beetle outbreaks. *Canadian Journal of Forest Research* 24:2089–2095.

Schmid, J. M., and R. H. Frye. 1977. *Spruce Beetle in the Rockies*. USDA Forest Service General Technical Report RM-49. Fort Collins, CO.

Six, D. L., and B. J. Bentz. 2003. Fungi associated with the North American spruce beetle, *Dendroctonus rufipennis*. *Canadian Journal of Forest Research* 33:1815–1820.

Veblen, T. T. 1986. Age and size structure of subalpine forests in the Colorado Front Range. *Bulletin of the Torrey Botanical Club* 113:225–240.

Veblen, T. T., K. S. Hadley, M. S. Reid, and A. J. Rebertus. 1991. The response of subalpine forests to spruce beetle outbreak in Colorado. *Ecology* 72:213–231.

Whipple, S. A., and R. L. Dix. 1979. Age structure and successional dynamics of a Colorado subalpine forest. *American Midland Naturalist* 101:142–158.

BIRDS, TREES, AND DEAD WOOD

Miller, E., and D. R. Miller. 1980. Snag use by birds. In *Management of Western Forests and Grasslands for Non-game Birds*, 337–356. USDA Forest Service General Technical Report INT-86. Ogden, UT.

STREAMS AND DOWNED WOOD

Livers, B., and E. Wohl. 2016. Sources and interpretation of channel complexity in forested subalpine streams of the Southern Rocky Mountains. *Water Resources Research* 52:3910–3929.

Livers, B., E. Wohl, K. J. Jackson, and N. A. Sutfin. 2018. Historical land use as a driver of alternative states for stream form and function in forested mountain watersheds of the Southern Rocky Mountains. *Earth Surface Processes and Landforms* 43:669–684.

OLD-GROWTH FORESTS

Rebertus, A. J., T. T. Veblen, L. M. Roovers, and J. N. Mast. 1992. *Old-Growth Forests in the Southwest and Rocky Mountain Regions: Proceedings of a Workshop*, edited by M. R. Kaufmann, 139–153. USDA Forest Service General Technical Report RM-213. Fort Collins, CO.

Robertson, P. A. 1992. Characteristics of spruce-fir and lodgepole pine old-growth stands in the Arapaho-Roosevelt National Forest, Colorado. In *Old-Growth Forests in the Southwest and Rocky Mountain Regions: Proceedings of a Workshop*, edited by M. R. Kaufmann, 128–134. USDA Forest Service General Technical Report RM-213. Fort Collins, CO.

WOOD DECAY

Herrmann, S., and C. E. Prescott. 2008. Mass loss and nutrient dynamics of coarse woody debris in three Rocky Mountain coniferous forests: 21 year results. *Canadian Journal of Forest Research* 38:125–132.

Kueppers, L. M., J. Southon, P. Baer, and J. Harte. 2004. Dead wood biomass and turnover time, measured by radiocarbon, along a subalpine elevation gradient. *Oecologia* 141:641–651.

Maser, C., and J. M. Trappe. 1984. *The Seen and Unseen World of the Fallen Tree*. USDA Forest Service General Technical Report PNW-164. Pacific Northwest Forest and Range Experiment Station, Portland, OR.

Mielke, J. 1950. Rate of deterioration of beetle-killed Engelmann spruce. *Journal of Forestry* 48:882–888.

WOOD-WIDE WEB

Beiler, K. J., D. M. Durall, S. W. Simard, S. A. Maxwell, and A. M. Kretze. 2009. Architecture of the wood-wide web: *Rhizopogon* spp. genets link multiple Douglas-fir cohorts. *New Phytologist* 185:543–553.

Wiemken, V., and T. Boller. 2002. Ectomycorrhiza: Gene expression, metabolism and the wood-wide web. *Current Opinion in Plant Biology* 5:355–361.

OTHER

Haskell, D. J. 2017. *The Songs of Trees: Stories from Nature's Great Connectors*. New York: Penguin Random House. (quotes from pp. 95 and 129)

Terwilliger, J., and J. Pastor. 1999. Small mammals, ectomycorrhizae, and conifer succession in beaver meadows. *Oikos* 85:83–94.

Lowlands

COASTAL DRIFTWOOD AND BEACH COMMUNITIES

Anderson, J. L., and I. J. Walker. 2006. Airflow and sand transport variations within a backshore-dune plain parabolic complex: NE Graham Island, British Columbia, Canada. *Geomorphology* 77:17–34.

Colombini, I., L. Chelazzi, and R. N. Gibson. 2003. Influence of marine allochthonous input on sandy beach communities. *Oceanography and Marine Biology: An Annual Review* 41:115–159.

Colombini, I., M. Fallaci, and L. Chelazzi. 2015. Ecological strategies of *Macarorchestia remyi* compared to two sympatric talitrids of a Tyrrhenian beach. *Acta Oecologica* 67:49–58.

Darnaude, A. M., C. Salen-Picard, and M. L. Harmelin-Vivien. 2004. Depth variation in terrestrial particulate organic matter exploitation by marine coastal benthic communities off the Rhone River delta (NW Mediterranean). *Marine Ecology Progress Series* 275:47–57.

Dugan, J. E., and D. M. Hubbard. 2010. Loss of coastal strand habitat in southern California: The role of beach grooming. *Estuaries and Coasts* 33:67–77.

Fairbanks, D. O., J. V. McArthur, C. M. Young, and R. B. Rader. 2018. Consumption of terrestrial organic matter in the rocky intertidal zone along the central Oregon coast. *Ecosphere* 9:e02138.

Gheskiere, T., M. Vincx, J. M. Weslawski, F. Scapini, and S. Degraer. 2005. Meiofauna as descriptor of tourism-induced changes at sandy beaches. *Marine Environmental Research* 60:245–265.

Kennedy, D. M., and J. L. D. Woods. 2012. The influence of coarse woody debris on gravel beach geomorphology. *Geomorphology* 159/60:106–115.

Pavesi, L., and J. Olese. 2017. Functional morphology and environmental adaptations of mouthparts in the driftwood amphipod Macarorchestia remyi (Schellenberg, 1950), and a comparison with the sandhopper Talitrus saltator (Montagu, 1808) (Amphipoda: Talitridae). *Journal of Crustacean Biology* 37:37–44.

Peinado, M., F. M. Ocana-Peinado, J. L. Aguirre, J. Delgadillo, M. A. Macias, and G. Diaz-Santiago. 2011. A phytosociological and phytogeographical survey of the coastal vegetation of western North America: Beach and dune vegetation from Baja California to Alaska. *Applied Vegetation Science* 14:464–484.

Porri, F., J. M. Hill, and C. D. McQuaid. 2011. Associations in ephemeral systems: The lack of trophic relationships between sandhoppers and beach wrack. *Marine Ecology Progress Series* 426:253–262.

Sakurai, I., and S. Yanai. 2006. Ecological significance of leaf litter that accumulates in a river mouth as a feeding spot for young cresthead flounder (*Pleuronectes schrenki*). *Bulletin of the Japanese Society for Fisheries and Oceanography* 70:105–113.

Schlacher, T. A., and R. M. Connolly. 2009. Land-ocean coupling of carbon and nitrogen fluxes on sandy beaches. *Ecosystems* 12:311–321.

Wiedenmann, A. M. 1998. Coastal foredune development, Oregon, USA. *Journal of Coastal Research* 26:45–51.

Wildish, D. J. 1982. Talitroidea (Crustacea, Amphipoda) and the driftwood ecological niche. *Canadian Journal of Zoology* 60:3071–3074.

Wildish, D. J. 2017. Evolutionary ecology of driftwood talitrids: A review. *Zoosystematics and Evolution* 93:353–361.

FOREST ANIMALS

Aubry, K. B., and C. M. Raley. 2002. Selection of nest and roost trees by pileated woodpeckers in coastal forests of Washington. *Journal of Wildlife Management* 66:392–406.

Burger, A. E., R. A. Ronconi, M. P. Silvergieter, C. Conroy, V. Bahn, I. A. Manley, A. Cober, and D. B. Lank. 2010. Factors affecting the availability of thick epiphyte mats and other potential nest platforms for marbled murrelets in British Columbia. *Canadian Journal of Forest Research* 40:727–746.

Forsman, E. D., and A. R. Giese. 1997. Nests of northern spotted owls on the Olympic Peninsula, Washington. *Wilson Bulletin* 109:28–41.

Hamer, T. E. 1995. Inland habitat associations of marbled murrelets in western Washington. In *Ecology and Conservation of the Marbled Murrelet*, edited by C. J. Ralph, G. L. Hunt, M. G. Raphael, and J. F. Piatt, 163–176. USDA Forest Service General Technical Report PSW-GTR-152. Albany, CA.

Hayes, J. P., and J. C. Gruver. 2000. Vertical stratification of bat activity in an old-growth forest in western Washington. *Northwest Science* 74:102–108.

Huff, M. H., N. E. Seavy, J. D. Alexander, and C. J. Ralph. 2005. Fire and birds in maritime Pacific Northwest. *Studies in Avian Biology* 30:46–62.

Johnson, M. L., and S. Johnson. 1952. Check list of mammals of the Olympic Peninsula. *Murrelet* 33:32–37.

Lock, P. A., and R. J. Naiman. 1998. Effects of stream size in bird community structure in coastal temperate forests of the Pacific Northwest, USA. *Journal of Biogeography* 25:773–782.

Parks, C. G., C. M. Raley, K. B. Aubry, and R. L. Gilbertson. 2007. Wood decay associated with pileated woodpecker roosts in western redcedar. *Plant Disease* 81. https://doi.org/10.1094/PDIS.1997.81.5.551C.

Ziegltrum, G. J. 2008. Impacts of the black bear supplemental feeding program on ecology in western Washington. *Human-Wildlife Conflicts* 2:153–159.

FOREST BIOGEOCHEMISTRY

Edmonds, R. L., T. B. Thomas, and R. D. Blew. 1995. Biogeochemistry of an old-growth forested watershed, Olympic National Park, Washington. *Water Resources Bulletin* 31:409–419.

Feller, M. C. 1977. Nutrient movement through western hemlock–western redcedar ecosystems in southwestern British Columbia. *Ecology* 58:1269–1283.

Fenn, M. E., C. S. Ross, S. L. Schilling, W. D. Baccus, M. A. Larrabee, and R. A. Lofgren. 2013. Atmospheric deposition of nitrogen and sulfur and preferential canopy consumption of nitrate in forests of the Pacific Northwest, USA. *Forest Ecology and Management* 302:240–253.

Keenan, R. J., C. E. Prescott, and J. P. Kimmins. 1993. Mass and nutrient content of woody debris and forest floor in western red cedar and western hemlock forests on northern Vancouver Island. *Canadian Journal of Forest Research* 23:1052–1059.

Kranabetter, J. M., S. M. Berch, J. A. MacKinnon, O. Ceska, D. E. Dunn, and P. K. Ott. 2018. Species-area curve and distance-decay relationships indicate habitat thresholds of ectomycorrhizal fungi in an old-growth *Pseudotsuga menziesii* landscape. *Diversity and Distributions* 24:755–764.

Luyssaert, S., E. D. Schulze, A. Borner, A. Knohl, D. Hessenmoller, B. E. Lawy, P. Ciais, and J. Grace. 2008. Old-growth forests as global carbon sinks. *Nature* 455:213–215.

Smithwick, E. A. H., M. E. Harmon, S. M. Remillard, S. A. Acker, and J. F. Franklin. 2002. Potential upper bounds of carbon stores in forests of the Pacific Northwest. *Ecological Applications* 12:1303–1317.

Sollins, P., C. C. Grier, F. M. McCorison, K. Cromack, R. Fogel, and R. L. Fredriksen. 1980. The internal element cycles of an old-growth Douglas-fir ecosystem in western Oregon. *Ecological Monographs* 650:261–285.

Turner, D. P., and E. H. Franz. 1985. The influence of western hemlock and western redcedar on microbial numbers, nitrogen mineralization, and nitrification. *Plant and Soil* 88:259–267.

Van Tuyl, S., B. E. Law, D. P. Turner, and A. I. Gitelman. 2005. Variability in net primary production and carbon storage in biomass across Oregon forests—an assessment integrating data from forest inventories, intensive sites, and remote sensing. *Forest Ecology and Management* 209:273–291.

FOREST CANOPY

Aubrey, D. A., N. M. Nadkarni, and C. P. Broderick. 2013. Patterns of moisture and temperature in canopy and terrestrial soils in a temperate rainforest, Washington. *Botany* 91:739–744.

Behan-Pelletier, V. M., M. G. St. John, and N. Winchester. 2008. Canopy Oribatida: Tree specific or microhabitat specific? *European Journal of Soil Biology* 44:220–224.

Berryman, S., and B. McCune. 2006. Estimating epiphytic microlichen biomass from topography, stand structure and lichen community data. *Journal of Vegetation Science* 17:157–170.

Clement, J. P., and D. C. Shaw. 1999. Crown structure and the distribution of epiphyte functional group biomass in old-growth *Pseudotsuga menziesii* trees. *Ecoscience* 6:243–254.

Dial, R. J., N. M. Nadkarni, and C. D. Jewell. 2011. Canopy structure in a 650-year Douglas-fir chronosequence in western Washington: Distribution of canopy elements and open space. *Forest Science* 57:309–319.

Edmonds, R. L., T. B. Thomas, and J. J. Rhodes. 1991. Canopy and soil modification of precipitation chemistry in a temperate rain forest. *Soil Science Society of America Journal* 55:1685–1693.

Franklin, J. F., and R. Van Pelt. 2004. Spatial aspects of structural complexity in old-growth forests. *Journal of Forestry* 102:22–28.

Ishii, H., and M. E. Wilson. 2001. Crown structure of old-growth Douglas-fir in the western Cascade Range, Washington. *Canadian Journal of Forest Research* 31:1250–1261.

Klopatek, J. M., M. J. Barry, and D. W. Johnson. 2006. Potential canopy interception of nitrogen in the Pacific Northwest, USA. *Forest Ecology and Management* 234:344–354.

Lindo, Z. 2010. Communities of Oribatida associated with litter input in western redcedar tree crowns: Are moss mats "magic carpets" for oribatid mite dispersal? In *Trends in Acarology: Proceedings of the 12th International Congress*, edited by M. W. Sabelis and J. Bruin, 143–148. Dordrecht, Netherlands: Springer.

Lindo, Z., and J. A. Whiteley. 2011. Old trees contribute bio-available nitrogen through canopy bryophytes. *Plant and Soil* 342:141–148.

Link, T. E., M. Unsworth, and D. Marks. 2004. The dynamics of rainfall interception by a seasonal temperate rainforest. *Agricultural and Forest Meteorology* 124:171–191.

McElhinny, C., P. Gibbons, C. Brack, and J. Bauhus. 2005. Forest and woodland stand structural complexity: Its definition and measurement. *Forest Ecology and Management* 218:1–24.

Nadkarni, N. M., and M. M. Sumera. 2004. Old-growth forest canopy structure and its relationship to throughfall interception. *Forest Science* 50:290–298.

Price, K., and G. Hochachka. 2001. Epiphytic lichen abundance: Effects of stand age and composition in coastal British Columbia. *Ecological Applications* 11:904–913.

Price, K., E. B. Lilles, and A. Banner. 2017. Long-term recovery of epiphytic communities in the Great Bear Rainforest of coastal British Columbia. *Forest Ecology and Management* 391:296–308.

Schowalter, T. D., and L. M. Ganio. 1998. Vertical and seasonal variation in canopy arthropod communities in an old-growth conifer forest in southwestern Washington, USA. *Bulletin of Entomological Research* 88:633–640.

Shaw, D. C. 2004. Vertical organization of canopy biota. In *Forest Canopies*, 2nd ed., edited by M. D. Lowman and H. B. Rinker, 73–101. Amsterdam: Elsevier.

Tejo, C. 2013. Canopy soils, litterfall and litter decomposition in a coastal old-growth temperate rainforest, Washington. PhD diss., University of Washington.

Van Pelt, R., and J. F. Franklin. 2000. Influence of canopy structure on the understory environment in tall, old-growth, conifer forests. *Canadian Journal of Forest Research* 30:1231–1245.

LARGE WOOD IN RIVER CORRIDORS

Abbe, T. B., and D. R. Montgomery. 1996. Large woody debris jams, channel hydraulics and habitat formation in large rivers. *Regulated Rivers: Research and Management* 12:201–221.

Abbe, T. B., and D. R. Montgomery. 2003. Patterns and processes of wood debris accumulation in the Queets River basin, Washington. *Geomorphology* 51:81–107.

Balian, E. V., and R. J. Naiman. 2005. Abundance and production of riparian trees in the lowland floodplain of the Queets River, Washington. *Ecosystems* 8:841–861.

Battin, T. J., K. Besemer, M. M. Bengtsson, A. M. Romani, and A. I. Packman. 2016. The ecology and biogeochemistry of stream biofilms. *Nature Reviews Microbiology* 14:251–263.

Borchardt, D. 1993. Effects of flow and refugia on drift loss of benthic macroinvertebrates: Implications for habitat restoration in lowland streams. *Freshwater Biology* 29:221–227.

Ciliak, M., T. Cejka, and J. Steffek. 2015. Molluscan diversity in stream driftwood: Relation to land use and river section. *Polish Journal of Ecology* 63:124–134.

Collins, B. D., D. R. Montgomery, K. L. Fetherston, and T. B. Abbe. 2012. The floodplain large-wood cycle hypothesis: A mechanism for the physical and biotic structuring of temperate forested alluvial valleys in the North Pacific coastal ecoregion. *Geomorphology* 139/140:460–470.

Crenshaw, C. L., H. M. Valett, and J. L. Tank. 2002. Effects of coarse particulate organic matter on fungal biomass and invertebrate density in the subsurface of a headwater stream. *Journal of the North American Benthological Society* 21:28–42.

Greenwald, D. N., and L. B. Brubaker. 2001. A 5000-year record of disturbance and vegetation change in riparian forests of the Queets River, Washington, USA. *Canadian Journal of Forest Research* 31:1375–1385.

Hax, C. L., and S. W. Golladay. 1998. Flow disturbance of macroinvertebrates inhabiting sediments and woody debris in a prairie stream. *American Midland Naturalist* 139:210–223.

Hyatt, T. L., and R. J. Naiman. 2001. The residence time of large woody debris in the Queets River, Washington, USA. *Ecological Applications* 11:191–202.

Latterell, J. J., and R. J. Naiman. 2007. Sources and dynamics of large logs in a temperate floodplain river. *Ecological Applications* 17:1127–1141.

Montgomery, D. R., and T. B. Abbe. 2006. Influence of logjam-formed hard points on the formation of valley-bottom landforms in an old-growth forest valley, Queets River, Washington, USA. *Quaternary Research* 65:147–155.

Naiman, R. J., J. S. Bechtold, T. J. Beechie, J. J. Latterell, and R. Van Pelt. 2010. A process-based view of floodplain forest patterns in coastal river valleys of the Pacific Northwest. *Ecosystems* 13:1–31.

O'Connor, J. E., M. A. Jones, and T. L. Haluska. 2003. Flood plain and channel dynamics of the Quinault and Queets Rivers, Washington, USA. *Geomorphology* 51:31–59.

Van Pelt, R., T. C. O'Keefe, J. J. Latterell, and R. J. Naiman. 2006. Riparian forest stand development along the Queets River in Olympic National Park, Washington. *Ecological Monographs* 76:277–298.

Ward, G. M., and N. G. Aumen. 1986. Woody debris as a source of fine particulate organic matter in coniferous forest stream ecosystems. *Canadian Journal of Fisheries and Aquatic Sciences* 43:1635–1642.

WESTERN REDCEDAR

Duffield, J. W. 1956. *Damage to Western Washington Forests from November 1955 Cold Wave.* USDA Forest Service Research Note 129. Pacific Northwest Forest and Range Experiment Station, Portland, OR.

Minore, D. 1990. *Thuja plicata*: Western redcedar. In *Silvics of North America*, 590–600. USDA Forest Service Agriculture Handbook 654. Washington, DC.

Murrill, W. A. 1914. An enemy of the western redcedar. *Mycologia* 6:93–94.

Nystrom, M. N., D. S. DeBell, and C. D. Oliver. 1984. *Development of Young Growth Western Redcedar Stands.* USDA Forest Service Research Paper PNW-324. Portland, OR.

O'Connell, L. M., K. Ritland, and S. L. Thompson. 2008. Patterns of post-glacial colonization by western redcedar (*Thuja plicata*, Cupressaceae) as revealed by microsatellite markers. *Botany* 86:194–203.

Parker, T. 1986. Ecology of western redcedar groves. Dissertation Abstracts International B:47, 1813-B.

Peng, D., and X. Q. Wang. 2008. Reticulate evolution in *Thuja* inferred from multiple gene sequences: Implications for the study of biogeographical disjunction between eastern Asia and North America. *Molecular Phylogenetics and Evolution* 47:1190–1202.

WOOD DECAY

Kim, Y. S., and A. P. Singh. 2000. Micromorphological characteristics of wood degradation in wet environments: A review. *IAWA Journal* 21:135–155.

Maser, C., and J. M. Trappe. 1984. *The Seen and Unseen World of the Fallen Tree.* USDA Forest Service General Technical Report PNW-164. Pacific Northwest Forest and Range Experiment Station, Portland OR.

OTHER

Cockroft, A. C., and A. McLachlan. 1993. Nitrogen budget for a high-energy ecosystem. *Marine Ecology Progress Series* 100:287–299.

DeBell, D. S., and J. F. Franklin. 1987. Old-growth Douglas-fir and western hemlock: A 36-year record of growth and mortality. *Western Journal of Applied Forestry* 2:111–114.

Edmonds, R. L., T. B. Thomas, and K. P. Maybury. 1993. Tree population dynamics, growth, and mortality in old-growth forests in the western Olympic Mountains, Washington. *Canadian Journal of Forest Research* 23:512–519.

Gavin, D. G., and L. B. Brubaker. 2015. The modern landscape of the Olympic Peninsula. In *Late Pleistocene and Holocene Environmental Change on the Olympic Peninsula, Washington*, 3–36. Cham, Switzerland: Springer.

Harrington, C. A., K. R. Buermeyer, L. C. Brodie, and B. W. Wender. 2002. *Factors Influencing Growth and Flowering of Understory Plants in Conifer Stands in Western Washington*, 159–168. USDA Forest Service General Technical Report PNW-GTR-563. Portland, OR.

Hessburg, P. F., R. G. Mitchell, and G. M. Filip. 1994. *Historical and Current Roles of Insects and Pathogens in Eastern Oregon and Washington Forested Landscapes*. USDA Forest Service General Technical Report PNW-GTR-327. Portland, OR.

Lock, M. A., R. R. Wallace, J. W. Costerton, R. M. Ventullo, and S. E. Charton. 1984. River epilithon: Toward a structural-functional model. *Oikos* 42:10–22.

Olafsson, E. 1982. *The Status of the Land-Arthropod Fauna on Surtsey, Iceland, in Summer 1981*, 68–72. Reykjavik: Icelandic Museum of Natural History.

Piercey-Normore, M. D. 2005. Lichens from the Hudson Bay Lowlands: Northeastern coastal regions of Wapusk National Park in Manitoba. *Canadian Journal of Botany* 83:1029–1038.

Piercey-Normore, M. D., I. M. Brodo, and C. Deduke. 2016. Lichens on the Hudson Bay Lowlands: A long-term survey in Wapusk National Park, Manitoba. *Lichenologist* 48:581–592.

Walker, I. J., and J. V. Barrie. 2004. Geomorphology and sea-level rise on one of Canada's most sensitive coasts: Northeast Graham Island, British Columbia. *Journal of Coastal Research* 39:220–226.

Traveler

BALSAM POPLAR

Adonsou, K. E., I. Drobyshev, A. DesRochers, and F. Tremblay. 2016. Root connections affect radial growth of balsam poplar trees. *Trees* 30:1775–1783.

Keller, S. R., M. S. Olson, S. Silim, W. Schroeder, and P. Tiffin. 2010. Genomic diversity, population structure, and migration following rapid range expansion in the balsam poplar, *Populus balsamifera*. *Molecular Ecology* 19:1212–1226.

MEDICINAL USES OF BALSAM POPLAR

Colantonio, S., and J. K. Rivers. 2017. Botanicals with dermatologic properties derived from First Nations healing: Part I—Trees. *Journal of Cutaneous Medicine and Surgery* 21:288–298.

RIVER AND LAKE DRIFTWOOD

Kramer, N., and E. Wohl. 2015. Driftcretions: The legacy impacts of driftwood on shoreline morphology. *Geophysical Research Letters* 42:5855–5864.

Kramer, N., and E. Wohl. 2017. Rules of the road: A qualitative and quantitative synthesis of large wood transport through drainage networks. *Geomorphology* 279:74–97.

Kramer, N., E. Wohl, B. Hess-Homeier, and S. Leisz. 2017. The pulse of driftwood export from a very large forested river basin over multiple time scales, Slave River, Canada. *Water Resources Research* 53:1928–1947.

Papik, R., M. Marschke, and G. B. Ayles. 2003. *Inuvialuit Traditional Ecological Knowledge of Fisheries in Rivers West of the Mackenzie River in the Canadian Arctic.* Canada/Inuvialuit Fisheries Joint Management Committee Technical Report Series, Report 2003-4. Inuvik, Canada.

MARINE DRIFTWOOD AND DEEP-SEA ECOSYSTEMS

Alix, C. 2005. Deciphering the impact of change on the driftwood cycle: Contribution to the study of human use of wood in the Arctic. *Global and Planetary Change* 47:83–98.

Blanchette, R. A., B. W. Held, L. Hellmann, L. Millman, and U. Buntgen. 2016. Arctic driftwood reveals unexpectedly rich fungal diversity. *Fungal Ecology* 23:58–65.

Caddy, J. F., and J. Majkowski. 1996. Tuna and trees: A reflection on a long-term perspective for tuna fishing around floating logs. *Fisheries Research* 25:369–376.

Distel, D. L., A. R. Baco, E. Chuang, W. Morrill, C. Cavanaugh, and C. R. Smith. 2000. Do mussels take wooden steps to deep-sea vents? *Nature* 403:725–726.

Doong, D. J., H. C. Chuang, C. L. Shieh, and J. H. Hu. 2011. Quantity, distribution, and impacts of coastal driftwood triggered by a typhoon. *Marine Pollution Bulletin* 62:1446–1454.

Dubilier, N., C. Bergin, and C. Lott. 2008. Symbiotic diversity in marine animals: The art of harnessing chemosynthesis. *Nature Reviews: Microbiology* 6:725–740.

Dunton, K. H., T. Weingartner, and E. C. Carmack. 2006. The nearshore western Beaufort Sea ecosystem: Circulation and importance of terrestrial carbon in arctic coastal food webs. *Progress in Oceanography* 71:362–378.

Eggertsson, O. 1994. Mackenzie River driftwood—a dendrochronological study. *Arctic* 47:128–136.

Emery, K. O. 1955. Transportation of rocks by driftwood. *Journal of Sedimentary Petrology* 25:51–57.

Fagervold, S. K., P. E. Galand, M. Zbinden, F. Gaill, P. Lebaron, and C. Palacios. 2012. Sunken woods on the ocean floor provide diverse specialized habitats for microorganisms. *FEMS Microbiology Ecology* 82:616–628.

Fagervold, S. K., C. Romano, D. Kalenitchenko, C. Borowski, A. Nunes-Jorge, D. Martin, and P. E. Galand. 2014. Microbial communities in sunken wood are structured by wood-boring bivalves and location in a submarine canyon. *PLoS ONE* 9:e96248.

Friesen, T. M. 2004. Kitigaaryuit: A portrait of the Mackenzie Inuit in the 1890s, based on the journals of Isaac O. Stringer. *Arctic Anthropology* 41:222–237.

Gooding, R. M., and J. J. Magnuson. 1967. Ecological significance of a drifting object to pelagic fishes. *Pacific Science* 21:486–497.

Hellmann, L., W. Tegel, O. Eggertsson, F. H. Schweingruber, R. Blanchette, A. Kirdyanov, H. Gartner, and U. Buntgen. 2013. Tracing the origin of Arctic driftwood. *Journal of Geophysical Research Biogeosciences* 118:68–76.

Hoyoux, C., M. Zbinden, S. Samadi, F. Gaill, and P. Compere. 2009. Wood-based diet and gut microflora of a galatheid crab associated with Pacific deep-sea wood falls. *Marine Biology* 156:2421–2493.

Kano, Y., H. Fukumori, B. Brenzinger, and A. Waren. 2013. Driftwood as a vector for the oceanic dispersal of estuarine gastropods (Neritidae) and an evolutionary pathway to the sunken-wood community. *Journal of Molluscan Studies* 79:378–382.

Khan, S. S., and P. Manimohan. 2011. Diversity and abundance of marine fungi on driftwood collected from Kerala State and Lakshadweep Islands, India. *Mycosphere* 2:223–229.

Kindle, E. M. 1921. Mackenzie River driftwood. *Geographical Review* 11:50–53.

McLeod, R. J., and S. R. Wing. 2007. Hagfish in the New Zealand fjords are supported by chemoautotrophy of forest carbon. *Ecology* 88:809–816.

Palacios, C., M. Zbinden, A. R. Baco, T. Treude, C. R. Smith, F. Gaill, P. Lebaron, and A. Boetius. 2006. Microbial ecology of deep-sea sunken wood: Quantitative measurements of bacterial biomass and cellulolytic activities. *Cahiers de Biologie Marine* 47:415–520.

Palacios, C., M. Zbinden, M. Pailleret, F. Gaill, and P. Lebaron. 2009. Highly similar prokaryotic communities of sunken wood at shallow and deep-sea sites across the oceans. *Microbial Ecology* 58:737–752.

Rama, T., M. L. Davey, J. Norden, R. Halvorsen, R. Blaalid, G. H. Mathiassen, I. G. Alsos, and H. Kauserud. 2016. Fungi sailing the Arctic Ocean: Speciose communities in North Atlantic driftwood as revealed by high-throughput amplicon sequencing. *Microbial Ecology* 72:295–304.

Rama, T., J. Norden, M. L. Davey, G. H. Mathiassen, J. W. Spatafora, and H. Kauserud. 2014. Fungi ahoy! Diversity on marine wooden substrata in the high North. *Fungal Ecology* 8:46–58.

Rice, M. E., H. F. Reichardt, J. Piraino, and C. M. Young. 2012. Reproduction, development, growth, and the length of larval life of *Phascolosoma turnerae*, a wood-dwelling deep-sea sipunculan. *Invertebrate Biology* 131:204–215.

Schwabe, E., I. Bartsch, M. B. Paszkowycz, N. Brenke, A. V. Chernyshev, N. O. Elsner, V. Fischer, et al. 2015. Wood-associated fauna collected during the KuramBio expedition in the North West Pacific. *Deep-Sea Research II* 111:376–388.

Shaw, J. D. 2008. Driftwood as a resource: Modeling fuelwood acquisition strategies in the mid- to late Holocene Gulf of Alaska. PhD diss., University of Washington.

Timoney, K. P., and A. L. Robinson. 1996. Old-growth white spruce and balsam poplar forests of the Peace River Lowlands, Wood Buffalo National Park, Canada: Development, structure, and diversity. *Forest Ecology and Management* 81:179–196.

OTHER

Fritz, M., J. E. Vonk, and H. Lantuit. 2017. Collapsing Arctic coastlines. *Nature Climate Change* 7:6–7.

Mars, J. C., and D. W. Houseknecht. 2007. Quantitative remote sensing study indicates doubling of coastal erosion rate in past 50 yr along a segment of the Arctic coast of Alaska. *Geology* 35:583–586.

Mazur, K. M., P. C. James, and S. D. Frith. 1997. Barred owl (*Strix varia*) nest site characteristics in the boreal forest of Saskatchewan, Canada. In *Biology and Conservation of Owls of the Northern Hemisphere*, edited by J. R. Duncan, D. H. Johnson, and T. H. Nicholls, 267–271. USDA Forest Service General Technical Report NC-190. St. Paul, MN.

Nanson, G. C., and H. F. Beach. 1977. Forest succession and sedimentation on a meandering-river floodplain, northeast British Columbia. *Journal of Biogeography* 4:229–251.

Perakis, S. S., and J. C. Pett-Ridge. 2019. Nitrogen-fixing red alder trees tap rock-derived nutrients. *Proceedings of the National Academy of Science* 116:5009–5014.

Rathburn, S. L., G. L. Bennett, E. E. Wohl, C. Briles, B. McElroy, and N. Sutfin. 2017. The fate of sediment, wood, and organic carbon eroded during an extreme flood, Colorado Front Range, USA. *Geology* 45:499–502.

Rowland, J. C., C. E. Jones, G. Altmann, R. Bryan, B. T. Crosby, G. L. Geernaert, L. D. Hinzman, et al. 2010. Arctic landscapes in transition: Responses to thawing permafrost. *Eos, Transactions of the American Geophysical Union* 91:229–236.

Spencer, R. G. M., P. J. Mann, T. Dittmar, T. I. Englinton, C. McIntyre, R. M. Holmes, N. Zimov, and A. Stubbins. 2015. Detecting the signature of permafrost thaw in Arctic rivers. *Geophysical Research Letters* 42:2830–2835.

Syvitski, J. P. M., C. J. Vörösmarty, A. J. Kettner, and P. Green. 2005. Impact of humans on the flux of terrestrial sediment to the global coastal ocean. *Science* 308:376–380.

West, A. J., C. W. Lin, T. C. Lin, R. G. Hilton, S. H. Liu, C. T. Chang, K. C. Lin, A. Galy, R. B. Sparkes, and N. Hovius. 2011. Mobilization and transport of coarse woody debris to the oceans triggered by an extreme tropical storm. *Limnology and Oceanography* 56:77–85.

Conclusion

Bernhardt, E. S., M. A. Palmer, J. D. Allen, G. Alexander, K. Barnas, S. Brooks, J. Carr, et al. 2005. Synthesizing U.S. river restoration efforts. *Science* 308:636–637.

Haskell, D. J. 2017. *The Songs of Trees: Stories from Nature's Great Connectors*. New York: Penguin Random House. (quote from p. 95)

Peipoch, M., M. Brauns, F. R. Hauer, M. Weitere, and H. M. Valett. 2015. Ecological simplification: Human influences on riverscape complexity. *BioScience* 65:1057–1065.

Ricciardi, A., and J. B. Rasmussen. 1999. Extinction rates of North American freshwater fauna. *Conservation Biology* 13:1220–1222.

Rockström, J., W. Steffen, K. Noon, A. Persson, F. S. Chapin, E. Lambin, T. M. Lenton, et al. 2009. Planetary boundaries: Exploring the safe operating space for humanity. *Ecology and Society* 14:32.

The Story of Deer Creek. n.d. USDA Forest Service. https://www.arcgis.com/apps/Cascade/index.html?appid=a1eab14df971439580ac2c17e308fa09.

Scientific Names

TREES
Aspen (*Populus tremuloides*)
Balsam poplar (*Populus balsamifera*)
Bigleaf maple (*Acer macrophyllum*)
Black cottonwood (*Populus trichocarpa*)
Black spruce (*Picea mariana*)
Douglas-fir (*Pseudotsuga menziesii*)
Engelmann spruce (*Picea engelmannii*)
Grand fir (*Abies grandis*)
Mountain alder (*Alnus incana*)
Necklace poplar (*Populus deltoides*)
Red alder (*Alnus rubra*)
Sitka spruce (*Picea sitchensis*)
Subalpine fir (*Abies lasiocarpa*)
Vine maple (*Acer circinatum*)
Western hemlock (*Tsuga heterophylla*)
Western redcedar (*Thuja plicata*)
White spruce (*Picea glauca*)
Willows (*Salix* spp.)

HERBACEOUS PLANTS AND WOODY SHRUBS
American cranberry bush (*Viburnum trilobum*)
Arctic cottongrass (*Eriophorum callitrix*)
Arctic white heather (*Cassiope tetragona*)
Arctic willow (*Salix arctica*)
Bearberry (*Arctous alpina*)
Bearberry honeysuckle (*Lonicera involucrata*)
Blueberry (*Vaccinium uliginosum*)

Bluejoint reedgrass (*Calamagrostis canadensis*)
Bog wintergreen (*Pyrola asarifolia*)
Bunchberry (*Cornus canadensis*)
Claspleaf twistedstalk (*Streptopus amplexifolius*)
Cranberry (*Vaccinium vitis-idaea*)
Crowberry (*Empetrum hermaphroditum*)
Currants (*Ribes* spp.)
Devil's club (*Oplopanax horridus*)
Dwarf whortleberry (*Vaccinium myrtillus*)
Fireweed (*Chamerion angustifolium*)
Highbush cranberry (*Viburnum edule*)
Horsetails (*Equisetum* spp.)
Mountain bluebell (*Mertensia ciliata*)
Northern bedstraw (*Galium boreale*)
Northern bluebell (*Mertensia paniculata*)
Northern red currant (*Ribes triste*)
Oregon grape (*Mahonia aquifolium*)
Pacific rhododendron (*Rhododendron macrophyllum*)
Prickly rose (*Rosa acicularis*)
Red baneberry (*Actaea rubra*)
Red huckleberry (*Vaccinium parvifolium*)
Red osier dogwood (*Cornus sericea*)
Ross avens (*Geum rossii*)
Salal (*Gaultheria shallon*)
Salmonberry (*Rubus spectabilis*)
Shrubby cinquefoil (*Potentilla fruticosa*)
Thimbleberry (*Rubus parviflorus*)
Willows (*Salix* spp.)

OTHER PLANTS
Cat-tail moss (*Isothecium myosuroides*)

INSECTS
Aspen leaf beetle (*Chrysomela crotchi*)
Bronze poplar borer (*Agrilus liargus*)
Carpenter ants (*Camponotus* spp.)
Forest tent caterpillar (*Malacosoma disstria*)
Gall midge (*Mayetiola thujae*)
Gray willow leaf beetle (*Pyrrhalta decora*)
Pacific dampwood termite (*Zootermopsis angusticollis*)

Poplar borer (*Saperda calcarata*)
Poplar and willow borer (*Cryptorhynchus lapathi*)
Satin moth (*Leucoma salicis*)
Spruce beetle (*Dendroctonus rufipennis*)
Spruce seedworm (*Cydia youngana, Laspeyresia youngana*)
Western cedar borer (*Trachykele blondeli*)
Western spruce budworm (*Choristoneura occidentalis*)

AMPHIBIANS
Giant salamander (*Dicamptodon copei*)
Northwestern salamander (*Ambystoma gracile*)
Olympic torrent salamander (*Rhyacotriton olympicus*)

FISH
Arctic grayling (*Thymallus arcticus*)
Bull trout (*Salvelinus confluentus*)
Chinook salmon (*Oncorhynchus tshawytscha*)
Coho salmon (*Oncorhynchus kisutch*)
Northern pike (*Esox lucius*)

BIRDS
American kestrel (*Falco sparverius*)
Bald eagle (*Haliaeetus leucocephalus*)
Bank swallow (*Riparia riparia*)
Barred owl (*Strix varia*)
Belted kingfisher (*Megaceryle alcyon*)
Black-and-white warbler (*Mniotilta varia*)
Black-throated gray warbler (*Dendroica nigrescens*)
Boreal owl (*Aegolius funereus*)
Brown creeper (*Certhia americana*)
Canada goose (*Branta canadensis*)
Chestnut-backed chickadee (*Parus rufescens*)
Common goldeneye (*Bucephala clangula*)
Common merganser (*Mergus merganser*)
Common nighthawk (*Chordeiles minor*)
Common raven (*Corvus corax*)
Downy woodpecker (*Picoides pubescens*)
Dusky grouse (*Dendragapus obscurus*)
Eastern screech-owl (*Otus asio*)

Flammulated owl (*Otus flammeolus*)
Flycatchers (*Empidonax* spp.)
Gray-headed junco (*Junco hyemalis caniceps*)
Gray jay (*Perisoreus canadensis*)
Greater yellowlegs (*Tringa melanoleuca*)
Great horned owl (*Bubo virginianus*)
Hairy woodpecker (*Picoides villosus*)
Hammond's flycatcher (*Empidonax hammondii*)
Harlequin duck (*Histrionicus histrionicus*)
Hermit warbler (*Setophaga occidentalis*)
House wren (*Troglodytes aedon*)
Hutton's vireo (*Vireo huttoni*)
Lesser scaup (*Aythya affinis*)
Marbled murrelet (*Brachyramphus marmoratus*)
Mountain bluebird (*Sialia currucoides*)
Mountain chickadee (*Poecile gambeli*)
Northern goshawk (*Accipiter gentilis*)
Northern spotted owl (*Strix occidentalis caurina*)
Northern three-toed woodpecker (*Picoides tridactylus*)
Nuthatches (*Sitta* spp.)
Olive-sided flycatcher (*Contopus cooperi*)
Ouzel (*Cinclus mexicanus*) ·
Pacific-slope flycatcher (*Empidonax difficilis*)
Pileated woodpecker (*Dryocopus pileatus*)
Pine siskin (*Spinus pinus*)
Raven (*Corvus corax*)
Red-breasted nuthatch (*Sitta canadensis*)
Red crossbill (*Loxia curvirostra*)
Red-tailed hawk (*Buteo jamaicensis*)
Ruffed grouse (*Bonasa umbellus*)
Sandhill crane (*Grus canadensis*)
Scoter (*Melanitta deglandi*)
Snowy owl (*Bubo scandiacus*)
Solitary sandpiper (*Tringa solitaria*)
Swallows (*Hirundo* spp. and *Tachycineta* spp.)
Tree swallow (*Tachycineta bicolor*)
Tundra swan (*Cygnus columbianus*)
Varied thrush (*Ixoreus naevius*)
Vaux's swift (*Chaetura vauxi*)
Violet-green swallow (*Tachycineta thalassina*)

Warbling vireo (*Vireo gilvus*)
Williamson's sapsucker (*Sphyrapicus thyroideus*)
Willow ptarmigan (*Lagopus lagopus*)
Wilson's warbler (*Wilsonia pusilla*)
Winter wren (*Troglodytes hiemalis*)
Wrens (*Troglodytes* spp.)
Yellow-bellied sapsucker (*Sphyrapicus varius*)
Yellow warbler (*Setophaga petechia*)

MAMMALS
American shrew-mole (*Neurotrichus gibbsii*)
Arctic fox (*Vulpes lagopus*)
Beaver (*Castor canadensis*)
Bighorn sheep (*Ovis canadensis*)
Black bear (*Ursus americanus*)
Black-tailed deer (*Odocoileus hemionus*)
Bobcat (*Lynx rufus*)
Canada lynx (*Lynx canadensis*)
Caribou (*Rangifer tarandus*)
Columbian black-tailed deer (*Odocoileus hemionus columbianus*)
Cougar (*Puma concolor*)
Deer mouse (*Peromyscus maniculatus*)
Elk (*Cervus elaphus*)
Ermine (*Mustela erminea*)
Grizzly bear (*Ursus arctos horribilis*)
Least chipmunk (*Neotamias minimus*)
Long-tailed weasel (*Mustela frenata*)
Marten (*Martes caurina*)
Mink (*Neovison vison*)
Montane shrew (*Sorex monticolus*)
Moose (*Alces alces*)
Mountain beaver (*Aplodontia rufa*)
Mountain goat (*Oreamnos americanus*)
Mountain vole (*Microtus montanus*)
Mule deer (*Odocoileus hemionus*)
North American porcupine (*Erethizon dorsatum*)
Northern collared lemming (*Dicrostonyx groenlandicus*)
Northern flying squirrel (*Glaucomys sabrinus*)
Pacific fisher (*Martes pennanti*)
Pine marten (*Martes americana*)

Pine squirrel (*Tamiasciurus hudsonicus fremonti*)
Polar bear (*Ursus maritimus*)
Porcupine (*Erethizon dorsatum*)
Raccoon (*Procyon lotor*)
Red-backed mouse (*Clethrionomys gapperi*)
Red fox (*Vulpes vulpes*)
Red tree vole (*Phenacomys longicaudus*)
Snowshoe hare (*Lepus americanus*)
Southern red-backed vole (*Myodes gapperi*)
Stone sheep (*Ovis dalli stonei*)
Striped skunk (*Mephitis mephitis*)
Western spotted skunk (*Spilogale gracilis*)
Wolf (*Canis lupus*)
Wolverine (*Gulo gulo*)

OTHER
Spruce broom rust (*Chrysomyxa arctostaphyli*)

Index